Yen-Po Fang

The Developing of Emerging Integrated Currency

Yen-Po Fang

The Developing of Emerging Integrated Currency

Asian Macroeconomic Issues, Artificial Neural Network

VDM Verlag Dr. Müller

Imprint

Bibliographic information by the German National Library: The German National Library lists this publication at the German National Bibliography; detailed bibliographic information is available on the Internet at http://dnb.d-nb.de.

Cover image: www.purestockx.com

Publisher:
VDM Verlag Dr. Müller Aktiengesellschaft & Co. KG, Dudweiler Landstr. 125 a, 66123 Saarbrücken, Germany,
Phone +49 681 9100-698, Fax +49 681 9100-988,
Email: info@vdm-verlag.de

Produced in USA and UK by:
Lightning Source Inc., La Vergne, Tennessee, USA
Lightning Source UK Ltd., Milton Keynes, UK
BookSurge LLC, 5341 Dorchester Road, Suite 16, North Charleston, SC 29418, USA

ISBN: 978-3-639-00172-3

Content

Table Content

Figure Content

Chapter 1. Introduction

1.1. Research background and motivation

Rome Treaty established the European Community (EC) in 1958. It started the development of European Union. The purpose of regional integration is to reduce the risk and cost connected with exchange rate and trade via single currency integration. Moreover, European Union has created customs union to diminish barrier of taxation and increased profits associated with political cooperation. In the wake of Robert Mundell (1999) proposed the idea of optimal regional integration, this concept accelerates the European Unit (EU) to be born. Despite the creation process of European Unit (EU) confronts a lot of challenges and negotiations, Euro was formally in circulation in 2002[1]. Later, the European Union extended its scale to Eastern Europe in 2004. The members of EU increase from fifty to twenty-five countries[2]. This could further verify the positive effect of implementing Euro to benefit each member of European Union. Single currency mechanism could decrease transition cost and instability of exchange rate. (Letiche, 2000, Dutta, 2002)

Regarding to regional integration with a great diversity issue of economic, exchange rate regime, political and culture among Asian countries, many Asian economic originations were established such as Association of Southeast Asian (ASEAN), Asia Pacific Economic Cooperation (APEC) and the Asian Monetary Fund (AMF). In light of the successful of Euro, a progressive signal for regional integration could provide more confidence for Asian countries to consider creating the Asian Currency Unit (ACU). Recently, China announces a switch of Renminbi's regime into flexible currency in July 2005, and demonstrates the constitution of a basket of eight major currencies from China's major trading partners. The reference basket components contain trade value, external debt and foreign direct investment etc[3]. Moreover, the Asian Development Bank plans to calculate the exchange index of ACU and adds Taiwan and Hong Kong to extend the scale to fifteen currencies in June 2006[4]. This stimulates our motivation to follow the constitution mode of EU to find out optimal basket components for ACU. The purpose is to increase the stability and efficient in terms of ACU operation to compete with Euro and US dollar zones.

One of the advantages of implementing Asian Currency Unit is to reduce the instability of exchange rate that may generate severe currency crisis. For instance, the Mexican crisis in 1994, the Asia crisis in 1997 and Russian crisis in 1998 yielded serious damage for countries economic when the currency crises were broke out. When we overlook the impairment condition in Asia after

---

[1] Source: BBC Online Network, (2001/12/5), "The process of Euro born: From ideal to reality". http://news.bbc.co.uk/hi/chinese/news/newsid_1600000/16009742.stm.
[2] Source: WTO Electronic Report, No.10, "The reason for EU extended toward easten and analyzed the meaning of political and economic".
[3] Source: Economic Daily (2005/8/11), "Which basket currencies that Renminbi take it into account".
[4] Source: First Finances Daily (2006/3/22), "ADB: To promote the Asian Currency Unit on June".

1

breaking out the Asia Flu in 1997, several Asian countries such as Thailand, Indonesia, Malaysia, Philippines and Korea were suffered in extreme harm in terms of over 30% depreciation of their currencies. Moreover, the most violent depreciation range for Indonesia is higher than 60%[5]. Others Asian countries' economic system whatever China, Singapore, Hong Kong or Taiwan are all confront acute brunt. Although Japan was suffered slight influence by the Financial Crisis, but she broke out the economic bubbles in early 1990 so as to reduce the financial aid capability. Furthermore, it prolongs recovering time for Japan from the Asia Flu. The causes for generating currency crisis were viewed as a critical economic topic. Generally speaking, the source of currency crisis could separate into three major causes based on currency crisis theory, inconsistent economic policy, self-fulfilling of investors, and contagion effect. Many researchers discuss the contagion effect, Eichengreen, Rose, and Wyplosz (1996), Glick and Rose (1999), Leonardo and Rodrigo (2001) and Rijckeghem and Weder (2001) analyzed causes of the contagion. They categorized some key factors such as trade linkage, financial linkage and macroeconomic similarity and analyzed the relative importance. The purpose is to reduce the probability of contagion happen by efficiently controlling contagion sources for authorities. Regarding the event of Asia Finance Crisis that enhanced the feasibility for Asian currency integration, previous researches associated with a context of ACU didn't analyze the contagion source for Asian countries. To diminish economic difference and increase political cooperation, we further study an efficient controlling and solving in contagion effect. We overlook each contagion cause and hope to improve economic developed stability and cooperation mechanism in Asia.

In light of the tendency of regional integration and globalization, the economic and trade relationship become closer among countries in Asia. In order to avoid the tremendous damage from international contagion effect, this study tried to analysis the main cause for contagion for ten countries in Asian. On the other hand, we would like to analyze optimal basket component in Asian Currency Unit to constitute more complete single currency system. We hope this study results could provide a valuable reference to accelerate the formation of Asian Currency Unit.

---

[5] Source: Wang, Ho-Sung, "The impact on Taiwanese firms in ASEAN four countries and response policy of government in terms of the Financial Crisis". National Policy Research Journal, vol. 2 (1998/03/21).

1.2. Research goal

This study utilizes ten Asian countries' data in Export Volume, Net Reverse and GDP per capita with varied weights simulates the past decade central rate of Asian Currency Unit. We employ Artificial Neural Network and GARCH Models to estimate the optimal components for ACU and further analyze several topics as follow:

I.   This study was tested the forecasting performance for ACU against ten Asian currencies by using Back-Propagation Network (BPN), Recurrent Neural Network (RNN) and Time-Delay Recurrent Neural Network (TDRNN). Moreover, we compare the results of ANN models with GARCH (1, 1) model in terms of forecasting performance for central rate of ACU.

II. Based on previous studies which related with ACU constitution, this work added new macroeconomic variables (such as the ratio of foreign direct investment to GDP and the ratio of external debt to GDP) to obtain models suitable for searching the best basket components for ACU. In order to further confirm the effectiveness for optimal components of ACU, we compare the empirical results of Back-Propagation Network (BPN) with Radial Basis Function Neural Network (RBFNN) model. The purpose is to verify the performance of ANN model.

III. In regard to employ Adaptive Network-Based Fuzzy Inference System (ANFIS) model, the goal is to estimate the relevant importance in contagion sources (such as trade linkage, financial linkage and macroeconomic similarity) for ten Asian countries providing useful information for government authorities dealt with the contagion crisis.

1.3. Research flow path

Based on research purpose of this study, we sort relative literatures and further select useful research models to implement empirical analysis as shown in figure 1.

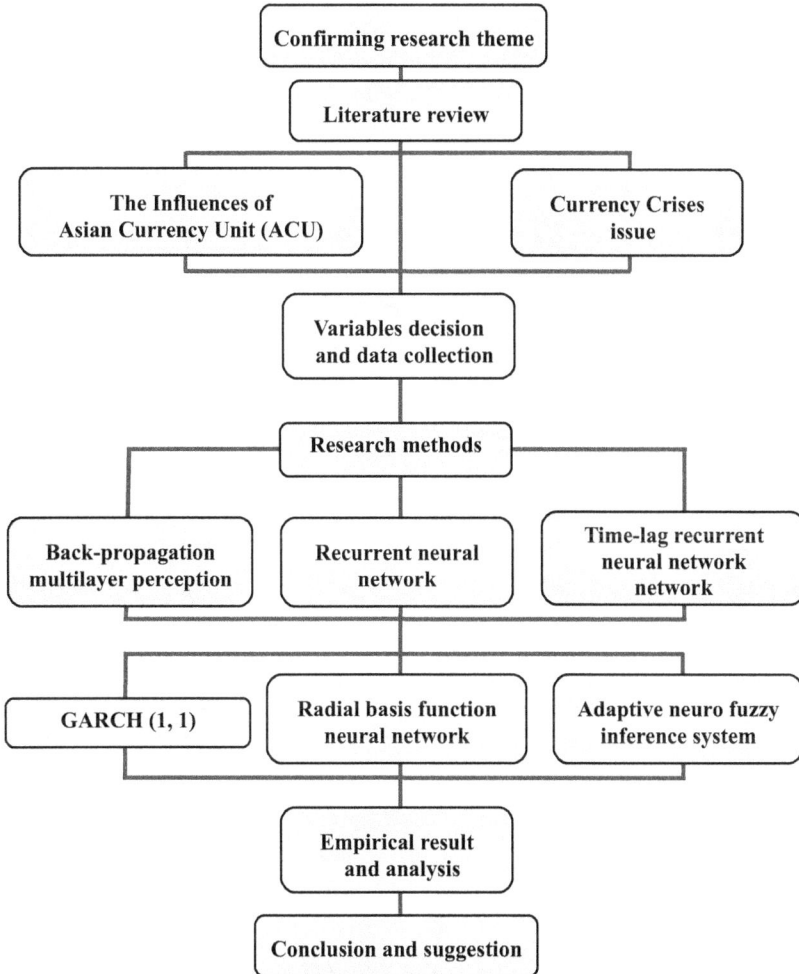

Figure 1. Research flow path

Chapter 2. Literature review

In first section, this work introduces the concept of Asian Currency Unit (ACU) briefly and demonstrates the related researches for regional economic topics. This investigation focused on the macroeconomic issue in terms of cause of contagion effect. Finally, we discuss about empirical methodology in this study included Artificial Neural Network (ANN) and GARCH models.

2.1. The Influences of Asian Currency Unit (ACU)

2.1.1. Asian Currency Unit (ACU) spring up

When this study overlooked the successful achievement of European Currency Unit (ECU) for past nearly five decades. Nowadays, more and more countries believe that the ECU could provide positive performance for their members. In light of this, the ECU could further prove the trend of integrating regional economy. The favorable experience for establishment process of ECU could provide an acceptable reference to Asian countries. However, the differences exist between Asian countries in terms of cultural, political issue and economic power countries (for example the war hatred). Those disadvantage factors which stated above make the regional integration becoming more difficult and challengeable in Asia. After the shock of Asian Financial Crisis in 1997, the majorities of economists and professionalism reconsider the possibility of establishing the Asian Currency Unit (ACU) and intensify interaction in economical activities.

The possibility of constituted Asian Currency Unit is feasible gradually emphasized by Mundell. It may bring tremendous economic benefits and vitality for global society. Based on Mundell's prediction, the economic capability of Asia will equally compete with Euro-zone and severely threaten to US-zone in 2020[6]. Yoshitomi Masaru, dean of the Asian Development Bank Institute in Tokyo, proposes an ideal of constituting the Asian Monetary Fund (AMF) in Asia. This mechanism could provide capital support of instable countries to avoid the occurrence of 1997 Financial Crisis again[7]. Likewise, Joseph Yam, Chief Executive of Hong Kong Monetary Authority, mentioned that an important reason for implementing the ACU[8] was to diminish severe volatility of Asian currencies.

There are several Asian regional development originations including the Association of Southeast Asian (ASEAN)[9], the Asian Monetary Fund (AMF)[10], and Asia Pacific Economic

---

[6] Source: Central News Agency, (2003/9/19), "Mundell: the economic capability of ACU-zone will equal to the Euro-zone in 2020."
[7] Source: Udndata.com, 2001; Economic Daily (2001/5/15), "Asia region principle spring up, looking for financial cooperation."
[8] Source: Udndata.com, 1999; Economic Daily (1999/1/06), "In case the Euro successful, it could hasten Global Currency Unit."
[9] The ASEAN was established in 1967. The original members included Malaysia, Indonesia, Thailand, Singapore, and Philippine. Brunei jointed in 1984. The members of ASEAN are ten countries until to now. Vietnam, Lao, Myanmar and Kampuchea following enter the ASEAN constantly after 1995. Source: Bureau of Foreign Trade.
[10] Japan proposed Asian Monetary Fund (AMF) this concept in 1997. Based on the members of ASEAN and plus Japan, China and South Korea, those countries provide 100 billion US. Dollars to be reserve fund. However, this concept was

Cooperation (APEC) to advance regional integration for Asia.

In 1967, the ASEAN was constituted in Bangkok. The group members of ASEAN are totally ten countries such as Thailand, Indonesia, Malaysia, Philippine, Singapore, Brunei, Vietnam, Lao, Myanmar and Kampuchea until to now. The ASEAN proposes the idea of Free Trade Area (AFTA). The purpose is to enhance the relationship of economic and trade among Asian countries. To enrich economic cooperation to whole Asia, the ASEAN invited China, Japan and Korea (ASEAN + 3 SUMMIT) to work out together for above perspective and to sign the Chiang Mai Initiative in Thailand since year 2000. In addition, the original members of ASEAN (Indonesia, Malaysia, Philippine, Thailand, Singapore and Brunei) carried out common effective tariff in 2002. Moreover, the ASEAN confirmed an agreement (Bali Concorde II) in Indonesia stated in 2003. The target is to convert the ASEAN into a European type of mutual economy system before 2020[11]. According to this agreement, it will create a single market with non-tariff barrier. The trade volume could approximately reach 700 billions per year. One of the ASEAN members, Malaysia suggested to switch the ASEAN summit into East Asia Summit (EAS) in June, 2004. This high level meeting was first been hosted on 14th December in Kuala Lumpur 2005. The inaugural East Asia Summit (EAS) is expected to drag ASEAN to tie relationships with China, Japan, South Korea, India, Australia, New Zealand and India[12]. Furthermore, China will establish the Free Trade Area with ASEAN in 2010 and Japan also will make a plan to constitute the Free Trade Area with ASEAN in 2012.

2.1.2. The researches for Asian Currency Unit (ACU)

In light of exchange rate of Asian currency researches, Raj and Mbodja (1996) estimated the currency relative influence power among Asian currencies and US dollar via long-term cointegration testing. The result indicates that Japanese yen have higher influence power than US dollar to other Asian currencies, including currencies of Taiwan, Hong Kong, Korea, Singapore, Malaysia, Philippines, and Thailand. This suggests that an international status of Japan was raising in recent years. Most importantly, the Asian economic and financial integrated extent is tighter than before. Tzeng (1999) estimates currency unit stability regards to Euro and further outlook the possible of Asian currency unit establishment. He mentions that if two countries exhibit high relative for exchange rate movement. It could provide positive favor for constituting an integration of currency unit. The research period covers from January 1991 to April 1999. Under the members of European Union that constituted the Euro, this process may provide suitable framework for

---

resisted by America and IMF. Japan proposed the idea of AMF again in 1998. America and IMF in favor to this 30 billion US. Dollars project.

[11] Source: Associated Press, 2003 "Constituted the mutual economy system in terms of Eurupoean mode. The Asian ten countries conduct new agreement". http://www.cdn.com.tw/daily/2003/10/08/text/921008h1.htm.

[12] Source: 11th ASEAN Summit Information Overview,

http://www.11thaseansummit.org.my/AboutSummit.php?PHPSESSID=c25d108720a327ff801cbfb770399fa4.

creating Asian Currency Unit. By setting up NT. Dollar to be one of the central currencies to establish optimal currency zone, the author strongly recommends that the Asian Union's members may include Taiwan, Indonesia, Korea, Malaysia, Philippines and Thailand according to correlation test. Those six countries have similar economy scale, providing best integration benefit for mutual currency.

In comparing regional currency agreement among the ASEAN, the Mercosur[13] and the NAFTA[14], Bayoumi and Mauro (2001) find that the economic scale and political condition of the ASEAN exhibit a larger difference from the other regional organization. To some degree, they suggest that the successful currency integration experience from EU could provide for conducting Asian currency integration. In addition, they also mention that it could be helpful to establish similar organization such as European currency union.

Various studies have analyzed the integration of Asian Currency Unit in recently years. Chen, Wang and Lin (2001) discuss that macroeconomic variables (such as money supply M1, inflation rate, current balance, government debt and short-term interest rate) influence to the central exchange of ACU and to analyze the extent of stability adjustment in central exchange rate of ACU. Chen (2001) considers the stability analysis of Asian Currency Unit establishment and the relationship between ACU with macroeconomic variables (such as short-term interest rate, customer price index and stock market index). Chen and Chen (2006) further analyze the relationship between Asian Currency Unit and monetary policy and constitute the target zone for ACU. Chen and Hsieh (2004) demonstrate the correlation research aspect of Asian Currency Unit and macro-trade variables. In addition, Hisao (2004) exerts Ordered Probit and Ordered Logit models to examine the threshold of currency crises.

In regard to probability of Asian currency unit establishing, Chen, Wang and Lin (2001) lead to begin the issue of central exchange rate of ACU. They used macroeconomic variables that influenced to the central exchange of ACU and analyzed the extent of stability adjustment in central exchange rate of ACU. They utilized Partial Adjustment Model and Seemingly Unrelated Regression Model via Panel Data Analysis and quoted exchange rate theory model which created by Somanath (1986). The ACU sampling from 1990 to 1999 totally ten currencies include Taiwan, Japan, South Korea, Hong Kong, Mainland, Singapore, Thailand, Philippines, Malaysia and Indonesia. In terms of effect of macroeconomic variables, inflation rate, current balance, government debt and short-term interest rate exhibit significant correlation with the exchange of

---

[13] Mercosur was established in January first, 1995 included Uruguay, Argentina, Paraguay and Brazil. Mercosur signs architecture agreement with EU in September 29, 1995 which becoming greatest trade group.
[14] NAFTA is abbreviation of North American Free Trade Agreement. The NAFTA was constituted by America, Canada and Mexico. This agreement was started in January 1994. The benefit of free trade area contain non-tariff barriers, import license, and import deposit etc.

ACU and could adjust the volatility of ACU rapidly. The other surprising results show that the relationship between ACU and Money Supply exhibit inverse variation in several countries such as Taiwan, Singapore, Malaysia, Thailand, Indonesia and Mainland. As a consequence, the adjustment speed will notably accelerate when covering the interval of Finance Crisis. This means that those macroeconomic variables could efficient control volatility of exchange rate to track it back to optimal interval.

In terms of stability analysis of Asian Currency Unit establishment, Chen (2001) considers the relationship between ACU with macroeconomic variables. She selects several variables, including short-term interest rate, customer price index and stock market index. The period of data collection is covered daily information from March 2, 1992 to June 30, 2000. The central exchange rate was consisted by currency exchange rate of ten Asia countries which included Taiwan, Japan, South Korea, Hong Kong, Malaysia, Singapore, Thailand, Philippine, Indonesia and Mainland against U.S Dollar and different weights of Export Volume, Net Reverse and GDP per capita. The mythologies contain ADF Unit Root Test, Granger Causality Test, Johansen Co-integration Test and Vector Error Correct Model. The results show that ACU will generate more serious volatility which influenced by short-term interest rate and trade from Japan. Policy makers can manipulate the stability of ACU in terms of controlling volatility of short-term interest rate so as to further decreasing the instability in macroeconomic operation in a wake of implementing ACU. In long-term forecast ability view, there are six countries exist long-term co-integration relation with ACU in short-term interest rate, CPI and stock index. In VAR impulse response test, all countries have showed stable convergence in a wake of lags two and have seven countries exhibited fully convergent at lags ten.

When it comes to the relationship between Asian Currency Unit and monetary policy, Chen and Chen (2006) used Unit Root Test, Causality Test, Johansen Co-integration Test and Vector Error Correct Model to examine the relations of ACU, customer price index, interest rate and money supply growth rate. The ACU was composed of ten Asian currencies including Taiwan, Japan, South Korea, Hong Kong, Singapore, Malaysia, Thailand, Philippine, Indonesia and Mainland and considered average weights of Trade volume, Foreign Reserve and Gross Domestic Production. They demonstrated two section periods of Asian Financial Crisis in 1997. Before crisis, the ACU was influenced by past value of itself, Malaysian CPI, Singapore's interest rate and Japanese interest rate. In the wake of crisis, the result showed that influence factors are lagged value of Mainland's interest rate, Malaysian money supply growth rate and CPI, Hong Kong's interest rate, and Singapore's interest rate and CPI. Meanwhile, regarding to establishing target zone for ACU, they utilized GARCH (1, 1)-MA (1) model to estimate the volatility. In order to avoid the target zone becoming invalid, they set up three times realignment of exchange rate so as to distinguishing totally four basis period. As a consequence, there can be categorized into five target zones. The superior economic system could be suit for interval of 0 to 2.25% such as Japan, Singapore, Hong Kong and Mainland. Taiwan is suitable for interval 2.25 to 6%. The others southern Asia countries exhibit wide interval for 15 to 20% or above.

Besides, in the correlation research aspect of Asian Currency Unit and macro- trade variables, Chen and Hsieh (2004) found that the ACU existed significant influence to three macro-trade variables (i.e. term of trade, volume of trade and trade balance), revealing that the volume of trade exhibited superior influence by ACU. Regarding to the result of long-term co-integration, the results showed that the ACU could fully interact with macro trade variables in Taiwan, Hong Kong, Indonesia, Philippines, Thailand and Mainland. Moreover, ACU appreciates will result in volume of trade to be reduced in South Korea, Thailand, Hong Kong, Indonesia and Mainland. Finally, based on analysis of Forecast Variance Decomposition, Taiwan's trade variables will influence more significant by ACU. On the other hand, macro trade variables in terms of Japan and Mainland China generate the greater effect to ACU. That is to say, these two countries play a crucial role in the field of ACU research.

Regarding to the currency crises warning model, Hisao (2004) exerts Ordered Probit and Ordered Logit models with random effect to examine the threshold of currency crises. The criteria for the threshold are based on speculative pressure index and exchange rate pressure index. In measuring speculative pressure index, the author totally establishes six types of thresholds which distinguish by ACU or each country's currency exchange against US dollars. In terms of forecasting accuracy for this study, Ordered Probit model represents high forecasting performance over 87%. In determining threshold, Hisao set up different weights to estimate inconsistent threshold. She definitely proves that macroeconomic variables such as CPI could occur in the probability of currency crisis that may reduce after establishing central rate of ACU. This result provides positive evaluation for constituting the Asian Currency Unit. The generating probability of Asian currency crises could efficiently reduced by establishing stable Asian Currency Unit. In terms of prediction ability of currency crises, the estimating threshold composed of consumer price index (CPI) and real interest rate may exhibit the more significant effect than the estimating threshold composed of each country's currency against US dollar. In order to reduce the occurrence of currency crisis, government could control these two variables to reach the goal of diminishing possibility of currency trouble.

Synthesizing above studies which related with constituting the optimal currency system in Asia, many of researchers already analyzed the formation mechanism of Asian Currency Unit. The results reveal that each currency's volatility could diminish via establishing single currency in Asia. To concern the negative impact in stock market and economic structure after constituting the Asian Currency Unit, the authority could stabilize stock market and economic condition by controlling short-interest. In this study, we would like to further analyze the completeness for selecting optimal components of Asian Currency Unit. The purpose is to fully express the basket calculation so as to accelerate the formation process for ACU. The cited literature is summarized in Table 1.

Table 1 Synopsis researches for Asian Currency Unit (ACU).

Researcher	Study subject	Empirical results
Raj and Mbodja (1996)	They estimated the currency relative influence power among Asian currencies and US dollar via long-term cointegration testing.	The result indicates that Japanese yen have higher influence power than US dollar to other Asian currencies. This suggests that an international status of Japan was raising in recent years. Most importantly the Asian economic and financial integrated extent is tighter than before.
Tzeng (1999)	He estimates currency unit stability regards to Euro and further outlook the possible of Asian currency unit establishment.	The author strongly recommends that the Asian Union's members may include Taiwan, Indonesia, Korea, Malaysia, Philippines and Thailand according to correlation test. Those six countries have similar economy scale, providing best integration benefit for mutual currency.
Bayoumi and Mauro (2001)	In comparing regional currency agreement among the ASEAN, the Mercosur and the NAFTA.	They suggest that the successful currency integration experience from EU could provide for conducting Asian currency integration. In addition, they also mention that it could be helpful to establish similar organization such as European currency union.
Chen, Wang and Lin (2001)	Discuss that macroeconomic variables influence to the central exchange of ACU and to analyze the extent of stability adjustment in central exchange rate of ACU.	In terms of effect of macroeconomic variables, inflation rate, current balance, government debt and short-term interest rate exhibit significant correlation with the exchange of ACU and could adjust the volatility of ACU rapidly. This means that those macroeconomic variables could efficient control volatility of exchange rate to track it back to optimal interval.
Chen (2001)	She considers the stability analysis of Asian Currency Unit establishment and the relationship between ACU with macroeconomic variables (such as short-term interest rate, customer price index and stock market index).	The results show that ACU will generate more serious volatility which influenced by short-term interest rate and trade from Japan. In long-term forecast ability view, there are six countries exist long-term co-integration relation with ACU in short-term interest rate, CPI and stock index. In VAR impulse response test, all countries have showed stable convergence in a wake of lags two and have seven countries exhibited fully convergent at lags ten.
Chen and Hiseh (2004)	They demonstrate the correlation research aspect of Asian Currency Unit and macro- trade variables.	The results showed that the ACU could fully interact with macro trade variables in Taiwan, Hong Kong, Indonesia Philippines, Thailand and Mainland. Macro trade variables in terms of Japan and Mainland China generate the greater effect to ACU.
Hisao (2004)	She exerts Ordered Probit and Ordered Logit to examine the threshold of currency crises.	She definitely proves that macroeconomic variables such as CPI could occur in the probability of currency crisis that may reduce after establishing central rate of ACU. This result provides positive evaluation for constituting the Asian Currency Unit. The generating

		probability of Asian currency crises could efficiently reduced by establishing stable Asian Currency Unit.
Chen and Chen (2006)	Analyze the relationship between Asian Currency Unit and monetary policy and constitute the target zone for ACU.	There can be categorized into five target zones. The superior economic system could be suit for interval of 0 to 2.25% such as Japan, Singapore, Hong Kong and Mainland. Taiwan is suitable for interval 2.25 to 6%. The others southern Asia countries exhibit wide interval for 15 to 20% or above.

Source: Organized by the Author.

2.2. Currency crises issue

Mohan, Uma, and William (2003) made two definitions for currency crises, the extreme depreciation in large movement connected with interest rate and the large depreciation over past general depreciation level. The majority of investors tend to change their manipulation rule to sell domestic currency and to buy foreign currency so as to generate arbitrage behavior. In light of this, we sort out three main reasons which causing the currency crises.

2.2.1. Inconsistent economic policy

Around 1970~1980, most of countries exerted fixed exchange rate regime. When currencies occurred overly appreciation and depreciation, central banks have been intervened in the exchange rate market to maintain the undulation range. Krugman (1979) argued that macroeconomic stable played a crucial role for currency crises occurrence. Due to the fact that overly expansion monetary policy, both trade deficit and fiscal deficit will lead to serious deduction of foreign exchange reverses. By further confirming this point, Krugman (1991) and Robert and Nancy (1997) indicated that the government must confront challenge from speculators under fixed exchange rate regime. The speculators know that flexible interval of the exchange rate in the long-term resulted in more worse exchange rate fluctuation after breaking out the currency crises.

Taking an example of Asia Currency Crisis in 1997, the crisis was started in Thailand in spite of its good economic situation around first half of the year. However, owing to the great deal of foreign capitals inflow and hot money in pre-1997 period, Thailand accepted the suggestion from IMF regard to depreciate the Thai currency. After devaluating the Thai to solve the problem of overstated currency, many of foreign investors manipulated a capital flight then accelerated the devaluation of Thai. The neighborhood of Thailand was also influenced by sharply depreciation of Thai. As a result, it leads to the Asian Currency Crisis[15].

2.2.2. Self-fulfilling

In previous review we focus on inconsistent economic policy, generally speaking, many of researchers view this cause, called first generation model. Another explaining reason is talk about

---

[15] "In the wake of Asia Financial Crisis, the each banking security system development of Asian countries."
http://www.tier.org.tw/APECC/hotnews/Discussion_Papers/wp9903.html

the confidence of investors and herd effect.

In terms of second-generation currency crisis, Flood and Marion (1996) try to revise the stand point from the causes of first-generation currency crisis so as to focus the currency crisis occurrence on self-fulfilling. They discuss on Mexico currency crisis from 1992 to 1995, indicating that the interest rate of US Bond is significantly lower than the Mexican Cete Bond. Under this situation, the investors exhibit low confidence for domestic currency and eagerly purchase other currencies. This behavior will cause foreign exchange reserves sharply decreasing. In other words, the investors expect currency devaluation result from government's incorporate policy or less confidence for investment market. Those considerations from investor's self-fulfilling trigger off a currency crisis. Jeanne (1997) analyzed the relation between self-fulfilling speculation and the fundamentals regarding to the case of the 1992-3 crisis of the French franc. He presented a model which allowed us to view self-fulfilling as a phenomenon resulting in macroeconomic and currency fluctuation under a fixed exchange rate. On the other hand, they demonstrated that their model shows an illustriously better outcome in terms of tracking the depreciation level of the French franc in 1992 to 1993 than a linear regression. To further discuss the influence of self-fulfilling speculation for other currency crisis, Bratsiotis and Robinson (2004) followed the theoretical framework and testing model from Jeanne (1997) to proof the existence of self-fulfilling speculation in the 1994 Mexican crisis.

In terms of herd behavior, Scharfstein and Stein (1990) demonstrated that herd behavior and investment exist interactive relation with each other. Some investors simply mimic other investor's decision, ignoring the private information that they have so as to cause the movement of stock market volatility. Kaminsky, Lizondo, and Carmen (1997) point out that herd behavior is difficult to forecast because it may happen in stable economic condition. More precisely, the general investors will also consider an impact of the political issue or natural disasters on the exchange rate changes. In case they expect the economic condition will to be worsen. The speculators will make a decision to sell the depreciating currency constantly causing more and more investors to follow this idea. As a consequence, currency crisis was broke out. By contrast, Choe, Kho and Stulz (1999) examine the impact of herding effect and found positive feedback trading on stock market in Korea. They use order and trade data form November 30, 1996 to December 31, 1997. The results show that it exhibits strong evidence of herding effect via foreign investors before the period of Asia Financial Crisis. However, the evidence of herding is fail during the crisis.

2.2.3. Contagion effect

In this part, we will consider the characteristic of currency crises which occurring via Contagion effect. This type of currency crisis spreads to neighboring countries through closer trade relationship. The great deal of capital outflows, just like domino effect[16], happens in the same regional that influenced the finances system subsequently. In regard to analyzing contagious currency crises, Eichengreen, Rose and Wyplosz (1998) utilize binary porbit model to estimate the factors of currency crises occurrence based on trade linkage and similar macroeconomic variables. The period of study covers thirty years which began from 1959, and extracts research data from 20 industrial countries. In measuring currency crisis, they constructed the index of exchange market pressure to test the probability of crises occurrence. They point out that the trade linkage exhibits superior contagion effect than another spreading channel and similarity macroeconomic condition. It further proved that closer relation of trade linkage resulted in spillover of currency crises.

Based on the discussion in regional currency crises, Glick and Rose (1999) found that currency crises caused dramatically damage in connection with one country's currency and banking system. Five different occurrences influenced currency trend which included (1) the disintegrated Bretton Woods agreement in 1971；(2) the disrupted Smithsonian Agreement in 1973；(3) the currency crisis of European Monetary System (EMS) from 1992 to 1993 ；(4) the meltdown of Mexico currency condition in 1994 ；and (5) the Asian financial crisis in 1997. The author used totally 161 countries, and determined the "first victim" or "ground zero" to further discuss the contagion effect among trade partners. The "first victim" are Germany in 1971 and 1973, Finland in 1992, Mexico in 1994 and Thailand in 1997. The empirical results demonstrated that the crisis will influence by trade and other macroeconomic variables such as the annual growth rate of domestic credit, the government budget as a percentage of GDP and the current account as a percentage of GDP.

As stated above, when it comes to the occurrence of contagious effect and discusses the causes of Asian currency crisis, Tatsuyoshi (2000) uses probit model to verify the causes which was proposed by the IMF. For example, the large number of external debt and current account deficit are playing a critical role in occurrence of currency crisis. In analysis of macroeconomic factors, the author implements comparative research for Frankel and Rose (1996), Eichengreen and Wypolsz (1996), and Glick and Rose (1998). As a consequence, the empirical results show that bilateral aggregate could exhibits more significant response in explaining the general currency crisis.

In order to further confirm the ideas from Eichengreen , Rose and Wyplosz (1996) and Glick and Rose (1998) who considered the strength of trade linkage in contagion of currency crises, Kenneth, Chao and Chou (2002) estimated the trade affinity among five East Asia countries include Thailand, Indonesia, Malaysia, Philippines and South Korea. They used elasticity of substitution of each country's export based on translog function to calculate the trade similarity. They utilized SUR model to estimate the long term relationship. As the result, South Korea exists higher elasticity of

---

[16] The domino effect is the concept of continuing responds in some change. For instance, the occurrence of Financial Crisis. A cumulative effect produced when one event sets off a chain of similar events.

export substitution with Thailand and Malaysia when South Korea was confronted serious impact during the currency collapse of the Thai Baht. On the other hand, Philippines exhibit relative lower elasticity of export substitution to Thailand reflecting a smallest impact by contagion effect among those Asian economies.

Following the idea from Van Rijkeghem and Weder (1999) who defined the concept of absolute and relative financial competition, Leonardo and Rodrigo (2001) find out the relative importance among three main channels for contagion occur such as trade linkage, neighborhood effect and financial linkage. As the empirical results in testing sovereign bond market and stock market, the financial competition effects appear relative importance to trade linkage and nationhood effects due to their explaining ability in contagion issue. To further consider the contagion incidence source, they used probit regression estimation. The three main origins are common bank leading effect, trade linkage and country macroeconomic features. More specifically, they viewed the contagion effect through common bank lenders are more important than others in spreading the Mexican, Thai, and Russian currency crisis. To enhance performance they recommend that one could employ BIS[17] data to represent the indicator of financial linkage.

Except for the idea of causing currency crises broke out by regional trade linkage and financial linkage, Harald and Stefanie (2003) expand this issue from regional level to global level. They focus on the eleven sovereign bonds market which denominated via daily spreads of US dollar, including three emerging countries in Central and Eastern Europe (such as Russia, Poland, Hungary), three countries in Latin America (such as Argentina, Brazil and Mexico) and the five countries in ASEAN. To show the contagion effect more explicit in different epochs before or after the Asian Crisis, the authors divided all period into tranquil period, crisis period, transition period and post-crisis period, respectively. The empirical result shows that the Asian Financial Crisis results in the original causality relation and generate new change pattern. In particular, the result supports that crossing continents also have existed the regional and global contagion effect.

Marais and Bates (2005) further investigate the shift of contagion effect between tranquil and crisis periods during 1997 to 1998. They focus on the type of currency crisis on sovereign debt market. In the wake of breaking the crisis, the result shows that the contagion effect links between countries and reveals closer causal relations among Asian five countries when comparing with tranquil period. In addition, they found that South Korea was damaged more severe through cross-country's contagion.

Combining those researches for contagion effect that we mention before, several researches

---

[17] The Bank for International settlements (BIS) is an international organization which fosters cooperation among central banks and other agencies in pursuit of monetary and financial stability. Its banking services are provided exclusively to central banks and international organizations.

have demonstrated the source of contagion which could attribute to three major channels such as macroeconomic similarity, trade linkage and financial linking. In particular, the trade linkage has greater contagious effect than the channel of macroeconomic similarity. Others further prove that the financial linkage is major channel for generating contagion. Based on those empirical result stated above, they utilize probit regression or multiple regression to be the empirical model. We consider the ANN models have better non-linear capture ability and its tremendous experience learning power. In light of this, we want to employ the artificial neural network to analyze the contagion source issue. The purpose is to find out more accurate source of contagion for Asian ten countries so as to increase economic restoration for each Asian country. We sort some of literatures for discussing currency crises in Table 2.

Table 2   Synopsis literatures for currency crises.

Researcher	Study subject	Empirical results
Eichengreen, Rose and Wyplosz (1998)	They utilize binary porbit model to estimate the factors of currency crises occurrence based on trade linkage and similar macroeconomic variables.	They point out that the trade linkage exhibits superior contagion effect than another spreading channel and similarity macroeconomic condition.
Glick and Rose (1999)	Based on the discussion in regional currency crises, to test the source of contagion in five different occurrences currency crises.	The empirical results demonstrated that the crisis will influence by trade and other macroeconomic variables such as the annual growth rate of domestic credit, the government budget as a percentage of GDP and the current account as a percentage of GDP.
Leonardo and Rodrigo (2001)	They used Probit model to analyze the relative importance among three main channels for contagion occur such as trade linkage, neighborhood effect and financial linkage.	The financial competition effects appear relative importance to trade linkage and nationhood effects in terms of their explaining ability in contagion issue.
Kenneth, Chao and Chou (2002)	They utilize SUR model to estimate the trade affinity among five East Asia countries include Thailand, Indonesia, Malaysia, Philippines and South Korea.	South Korea exist higher elasticity of export substitution with Thailand and Malaysia When South Korea was confronted serious impact during the currency collapse of the Thai Baht.
Marais and Bates (2005)	They investigate the shift of contagion effect between tranquil and crisis periods during 1997 to 1998.	The result shows proved the contagion effect through link between countries and it reveals closer causal relation among Asian five countries when comparing with tranquil period.

Source: Organized by the Author.

Chapter 3. Empirical methodology

The purposes for this research are focus on the issues of forecasting for Asian Currency Unit and the causation of contagion effect. We utilized a popular forecasting technique, the artificial neural network and GARCH models. Reviewing the development for the ANN models, Rosenblatt (1958) first proposed "Perceptrons" which open a research road for different fields. Rumelhart and McClelland (1986) raised error back propagation algorithm and back-propagation network (BPN). Their contribution created new milestone for the ANNs. To enhance mapping capability, Powell (1987) simulated partial adjustment ability for human brain to propose Radial Basis Function Network (RBFN). The advantage for this model was to extremely reduce learning time. Time-Delay Neural Network (TDNN) belonged to feedforward networks. It solves stationary process problems such as pattern recognition study without considering time factor. (Weibel et al. 1989)

Except for several different neural networks as stated above (such as BPN, RBFN, and TDNN), the most general dynamic neural network called Recurrent Neural Network (RNN). The RNN allows that information could transmit reciprocally between neurons. This benefit could increase simulation stability and convergence time. The most famous architectures of RNN model such as Hopfield neural network, HNN (Hopfield, 1982, 1984) and Hopfield-Tank neural network, NTN (Hopfield and Tank, 1985). Hecht-Nielsen (1990) proposed Counter-propagation Netowrk (CPN) and its the network architecture could separate two parts, Kohonen network to classify input data and Grossberg network to constitute look-up table based on output value. Using desired output to map into hidden layer's nodes directly and then revises the connection weights. Furthermore, the Adaptive Network-Based Fuzzy Inference System (ANFIS) was proposed by Jang (1993). He combined the Fuzzy logic with features of artificial neural network. More specifically, this model constitutes the Fuzzy Inference System upon artificial neural network. The advantages are clear to demonstrate the optimal solution and containing robust learning ability simultaneously.

3.1. Artificial neural network (ANN)

Artificial neural network possesses parallel computation capability in line with the consideration of neural structure of human being. The most unique characteristic is that the ANN models are equipped with non-linear structure and non-assumption limitation for implementing. In addition, due to the ANN models exhibit greater learning ability through regulative learning algorithm and recursive interaction with environmental information. The ANN models are widely utilized for forecasting and classification. (Hawley, et al. 1990; Joseph, William and Hennie, 1998; Hu and Christos, 1999; and Chang, Huang 2003)

In forecasting to related macroeconomic indexes, Greg (2001) forecasts the Canadian GDP growth by using time series and neural network models. The monetary and financial variables included US and Canadian interest rate yield spread, the real 90-day corporate paper rate, the growth rates of real narrow (M1) and broad (M2) monetary aggregates, and the growth rate of real stock prices. The empirical results revealed that the neural network exhibits superior than other models. The ANN equipped with notable effect of long-term macroeconomic variables prediction to forecast the GDP growth. Massimliano (2004) used the same foresting tool to conduct macroeconomic variables prediction in EMU by comparing three different models (i.e. univariate linear, time-varying and non-linear models). There are 15 variables including real GDP, personal consumption and government consumption, investment and inventories, import and export, consumer prices, and the GDP deflator, unit labor cost, and unemployment, short-term and long-term interest rates, and real exchange rate and the trade balance. The most important finding is that ANN models show the best performance in the real exchange rate forecasting than others linear or pooling models.

In light of utilizing the ANNs model in finance field, there are several studies implemented bankruptcy prediction. Odom and Sharda, (1990) and Eric et al. (1996) have compared the predictive capability of the back-propagation and multivariate discriminant analysis model. They accepted the idea from Stornetta and Huberman (1988) to set up the binary inputs and output to be incorporating a range of $\left[-\dfrac{1}{2}, +\dfrac{1}{2}\right]$. It reduces the convergence time about 30 percent to 50 percent[18]. The result shows that modification of output value has extremely superior performance than the general back-propagation. In regard to predicting the performance of finance, Monica (2003) adopted to combine fundamental and technical analysis via neural network in financial performance prediction. The prediction capability of neural network is much better when weight against the minimum benchmark level in all experimental results. A rule extraction skill to improve learning ability of neural networks could notably enhance forecasting performance.

There are many researchers to analyze and forecast the performance of stock index. Jorge and Salvador (2005) estimated the forecasting performance of daily returns on the Spanish Ibex-35 stock index through comparing the Time series model, the smooth transition autoregression (STAR) models and artificial neural network (ANN). The results show that the ANN exhibits the best forecasting performance in terms of stock return. The results also demonstrated that the ANN models exhibited better outcome underlying Sharpe risk-adjusted ratio and mean net return in one-step-ahead forecasts. In line the similar empirical results with Jorge and Salvador (2005), Samanta and Bordoloi (2005) gathered daily details from three different indices, namely, BSE-Sensex, BSE-100 and S&P CNX Nifty in India. The data period covers from January 1999 to August 2000. They compared the ANN with the random walk (RW) in terms of their forecasting

---

[18] Stornetta and Huberman (1988) manipulated the output values as $OUT = -\dfrac{1}{2} + \dfrac{1}{\left(1 + e^{-NET}\right)}$.

accuracy. Incontrovertibly, the result indicates that the predominance of ANN models over their counterpart of RW.

In this study, our priority is to focus on the forecasting performance, accuracy of exchange rate and contagion influence factors. The artificial neural networks are equipped with tremendously learning ability. In light of this, we would like to draw support from the advantage of Artificial Neural Network (ANN) to reach our researching goal.

The artificial neural network model was established in 1957. The first ANN model is perceptron which was raised by Rosenblatt (1958). Many of researchers combine the ANN with other analysis tools. There are several different ANN models were utilized in engineering or hydrological fields. In recent years, the ANN methods were widely used in finances issue. However, most of studies are focus on stock market prediction relatively more than to discuss exchange rate forecasting by using the ANN models. Thus, it still exists a lot of research space for exchange rate prediction via the ANN models.

To analyze the tendency of exchange rate by utilizing the artificial neural network (ANN), Hu and Christos (1999) improved forecasting performance of several conditional volatility models to combine with ANN and further to examine the exchange rate of European Monetary System (EMS). The conditional volatility models included GARCH (1, 1), EGARCH (1, 1), IGARCH (1, 1) and MAV model. They put the data from these four volatility models into first layer of multilayer perceptron (MLP). The combined forecast value shows in output layer. The data was searched from Datastream which was comprised of 15-years daily exchange rates from the establishment of the European Monetary System on March 13, 1979 to December 30, 1994. The ANN exhibits high forecast performance in the crisis period and it declared superior to other linear combining models.

3.1.1. Back-propagation multilayer perception (BPN)

By using several predicting techniques such as general regression neural network (GRNN), multi-layered feedforward network (MLEN), multivariate transfer function and random walk models, Leung, Chen and Daouk (2000) discuss the forecasting accuracy for exchange rate. The data select from the monthly exchange rate of Canadian dollar, Japanese yen and British pound. The empirical results revealed that the GRNN models have better capability to diminish the uncertainty from nonlinear problems, showing a superior performance of forecasting currency movements. Based on several variables including money supply, short-term interest rate, industrial production index and long-term bond yield, Yeh (2002) applied back-propagation neural network model to implement forecasting performance of the Euro dollars. The result shows that the back-propagation neural network has better forecasting performance than generally regression models. To obtain a best BPN forecasting mode, Nieh, Fung and Ku (2001) analyzed variance of exchange rate for N.T. dollars against U.S. dollars. They determined best BPN model in terms of hidden nodes, hidden layers numbers, maximum epochs and learning rate. The testing model for parameters selecting contains original 14 variables which first proposed by Rauscher (1997). In a wake of deciding best parameter mode, the authors try to add new factors into original model such as interest rate, trade amount in the market and amount of balance account. The result shows that the original model which proposed by Rauscher (1997) indicated the better forecasting performance and explanation ability than adding new variables' model from their decision.

When it comes to evaluate the currency options, Chang (2004) compares the forecasting performance between back-propagation neural network and recurrent neural network. He utilizes four different volatilities such as GARCH volatility, historical volatility, implied volatility and non-volatility to be inputs for the ANN models. This research follows the currency option evaluation model from Garman and Kohlhagen (1983) to select the variables including the Euro, risk-free interest rate for Euro, and the closing price of Euro currency option from the PHLX. The study period is covered from January first 2001 to December 31 2003. As a result, the implied volatility exhibits the smallest forecasting error in both kinds of neural network. The variables selection caused significantly different influence in terms of choosing neural network types.

In first part, we use multilayer perception model to conduct forecasting for Asian Currency Unit (ACU). We calculated ACU data to constitute the general framework. Then we put out-of-sample into this general model which we already set up before. The forecasting results will be compared with GARCH (1, 1) model. Secondly, we would like to further examine which macroeconomic variables have significant influence power to establish the central rate of Asian Currency Unit. Except for previous research results for ACU establishment, our testing model contains other input variables such as the ratio of external debt to GDP, the ratio of foreign direct investment to GDP and the ratio of bank's on the private sector to GDP. The external debt could estimate a country's vulnerability when the country confronts external shocks. If the ratio of external debt to GDP is high, it means country may lack of repay ability so as to more early occurring currency depreciation situation. (Mark, et al. 1998) The foreign direct investment is measure the extent of exchange rate volatility. The ratio of bank's claims on the private sector to GDP could response a country's health condition for the domestic banking system. The final results were evaluated by using some estimating criteria such as Mean-Square Error (MSE) and Normalized mean-square error (NMSE).

This basic ANN model is composed of one input layer, one hidden layer and one output layer. Each input variable could represent by one node. The equally important idea is that each layer could contain several neurons. The multilayer perception model belongs to the feed-forward neural network and supervised learning. The model structure shows in depicted Figure 2. In learning algorithm part, the Multilayer perception (MLP) collocates with error back propagation algorithm.

19

In light of this back-propagation learning method, inference output value from MLP was called D_j, and compare it with actual output value, A_j. Generating gap between these two values will transmit back to forward layer so as to adjusting connection weight for MLP model. This method eliminates the divergence between desired value and actual value. On the other hand, it could also achieve learning effectiveness. The equation (3.1) represents the computation mode. In order to obtain the best solution for error function, we exert steepest descent method to complete this purpose. (Joseph, William and Hennie, 1998)

$$E = \frac{1}{2} \sum_j \left(A_j - D_j \right)^2, \tag{3.1}$$

where E represents error function, A_j represents actual output value from output layer, and D_j represents desired output value from output layer.

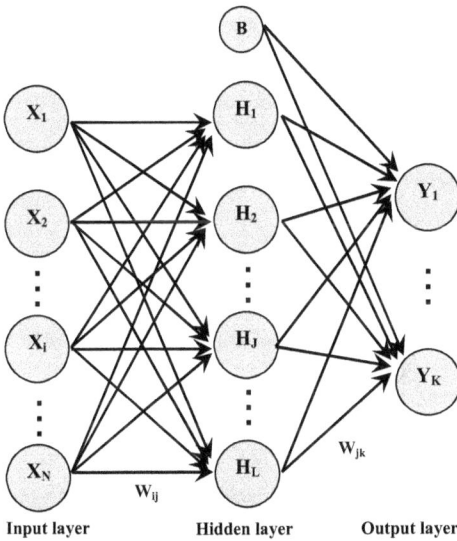

Source: Theory and Practice of Artificial Neural Network. (Chang Fi-John and Huang Hau Lung, 2003)
Note: A general structure for multilayer perception with a single hidden layer and single output layer; each line exist individual weight.

Figure 2. The architecture of MLP

In regard to link weights of computing process, relative weight plays a connection role for each layer. Figure 3 represents the linkage weights of calculation process. The function φ represents the *activation function* (Joseph, William and Hennie, 1998; Chang and Huang, 2003). Input values enter hidden layer and receive the linkage weights subsequently. In the wake of implementing summation linkage weights through activation function, as a consequence, it could convert to output value.

Sigmoid function is quite often taken to be the activation function. Equation 3.2 shows as following:

$$f(x) = \frac{1}{1 + \exp(-\alpha x)}.$$ (3.2)

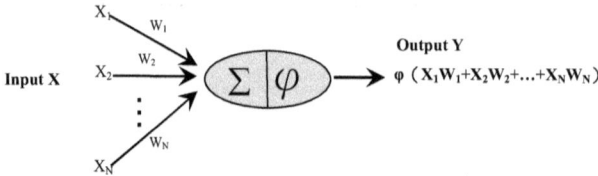

Source: Theory and Practice of Artificial Neural Network. (Chang Fi-John and Huang Hau Lung, 2003)

Figure 3. Graphical demonstration weights link process of neuron

As stated above, when we establish an ANN model there are several parameters that we need to consider cautiously, including the numbers of hidden layer's node, learning speed, and momentum parameter. The more hidden nodes exhibited better forecasting performance than the lesser hidden node's model. However, it required a longer convergence time. In light of previous empirical findings such as Tang and Fishwick (1993), Cybenko (1989), Kuan and White (1994), the ANN models have superior forecasting performance when the number of hidden nodes equal to the number of input nodes. (Tang and Fishwick, 1993). Following the suggestion of Cybenko (1989) and Kuan and White (1994), we exert one single hidden layer since this model has predominant performance for most economic requisitions. In case to add more hidden nodes or hidden layers can affect result in over-fitting and inferior forecasting outcome.

Learning speed plays a crucial role for the feed-forward neural network, because its learning ability could find and adjust more suitable value for the linkage weight. More specifically, the learning rate could decide degree of adjustment for the gradient steepest descent approach in the equation (3.3).

$$\Delta W_{ij} = -\eta \cdot \frac{\delta E}{\delta W_{ij}},$$ (3.3)

where η means the learning speed. We could further decompose $\dfrac{\delta E}{\delta W_{ij}}$ via chain rule. The equation (3.4) shows the manipulation process regard to linking weight in back-propagation algorithm.

$$\frac{\delta E}{\delta W_{ij}} = -\delta_j^n \cdot y_i^{n-1},$$ (3.4)

where W_{ij} denotes the weighted connection between the ith neuron in the input layer and the jth neuron in the hidden layer,

$\delta_j^n = W_{ij}$ represents the difference of linking above layer's nodes,

$y_i^{n-1} = W_{ij}$ represents the output value of linking above layer's nodes.

Finally, to avoid the local minimum generating, we will set up the momentum value α to maintain momentum among different weight change. On the other hand, based on empirical experience from Kecman (2001) and Yeh (2002), the most suitable selecting range for learning speed from 0.1 to 1.0 which could enhance the effect of convergence.

3.1.2. Recurrent neural network (RNN)

In this part, we use recurrent neural network model and time-delay recurrent neural network model to conduct forecasting for Asian Currency Unit (ACU). The ACU data was been calculated to constitute the general framework. Then we put out-of sample into this general model which we already set up before. The forecasting results will be compared with GARCH (1, 1) model. In light of the RNN and TDRNN models possessed the ability to consider the time-varying information, the RNNs also contain feedback and feedforward connections which equipped with great forecasting performance in long-term, provided greater dynamic adaptation capability for data's temporal memory. (Williams and Zipser 1989; Cohen et al. 1995; Mandic and Chambers, 2001; Chang and Huang, 2003) In order to deal with complex issue of exchange rate volatility, we would like choose the RNNs model to replace the static neural network.

In terms of the architecture of recurrent neural network, the RNN belongs to a multilayer perceptron. The structure contains three major layers, first one is concatenated input-output layer, second one is processing layer and third layer calls output layer. When the information $Y(t)$ was generated from processing layer, except for transferring into output layer, $Y(t)$ will transmit back concatenated input-output layer with time delay and connect with input value $X(t+1)$. Besides, concatenated input-output layer and processing layer required full connection. The structure shows as in Figure 4:

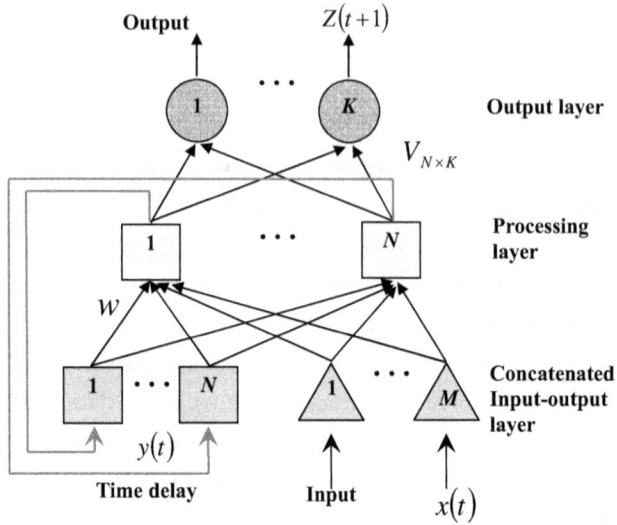

Source: Theory and Practice of Artificial Neural Network. (Chang Fi-John and Huang Hau Lung, 2003)

Figure 4. The Architecture for the RNNs model

In regard to the learning algorithm of RNN model, generally, we will utilize the Real Time Recurrent Learning (RTRL) algorithm to train the RNN. (Williams and Zipser 1989) We describe the error function in time t as follows:

$$E(t) = \frac{1}{2}\sum (d_k(t) - z_k(t)),\tag{3.5}$$

where $d_k(t)$ represents the desired value for the neuron, and $z_k(t)$ denotes the actual value. After using the steepest descent method, we can receive that the correction of connection weight is $\Delta v_{kj}(t)$.

$$\Delta v_{kj}(t) = -\eta_1 \frac{\partial E(t)}{\partial v_{kj}(t)},\tag{3.6}$$

where η_1 is the learning rate and $E(t)$ represents error function. We use chain rule to decompose equation (3.6) and find out the correction of $w_{mn}(t)$ via the descent gradient rule.

$$\Delta w_{mn}(t-1) = -\eta_2 \frac{\partial E(t)}{\partial w_{mn}(t-1)} = -\eta_2 \frac{\partial net_j(t)}{\partial w_{mn}(t-1)},\tag{3.7}$$

where η_2 represents the learning rate and this value would be allow different with η_1. We could receive the value of $net_j(t)$ by multiply the input value with the weighted connection. To determine Δw_{mn} by using chain rule again and m represents input numbers, n illustrates the number of recurrent neuron, and we can get evaluation equation as follows:

$$\frac{\partial net_j(t)}{\partial w_{mn}(t-1)} = \sum w_{ji}(t-1)\frac{\partial u_i(t-1)}{\partial w_{mn}(t-1)} + \sigma_{mj}u_n(t-1).$$ (3.8)

where σ_{mj} denotes the Kronechker delta function. (Blanco et al. 2000)

3.1.3. Time-delay recurrent neural network (TDRNN)

Time delay recurrent neural network (TDRNN) is an extensive neural model from traditional recurrent neural network. The TDRNN equipped with the advantages of adaptive time delays and recurrences. The adaptive time delays could help the network to choose useful information with time lags for the temporal correlations and prediction in the input sequence. On the other hand, the recurrences could enhance the learning ability and integrate temporal context information of sequences for the network. In light of the applicative advantages of TDRNNs superior than RNNs, it contains the shorter training time for convergence, and greater performance in catching the temporal location. The TDRNNs model didn't need large network size and additional hidden neurons to implement time delay analysis. (Cohen et al. 1995; Kim 1998)

The architecture of the TDRNN is shown in Figure 5. This neural network manipulates the temporal information of input sequences by employing adaptive time delays and recurrent connections. The TDRNN mainly comprised of five-layers and has an internal state layer. The internal state units act as the additional inputs at time t. it copies from the activations of the hidden units at time t-1. The network has modifiable synaptic weights and modifiable time lags via interconnections between the input unit and hidden units while both time delays and weights are adjusted. The *delay box* constitutes of interconnections from the input layer to the first hidden layer and also from the internal state layer to the first hidden layer. We select sigmoid function to be the activation function for this part. (Kim 1998)

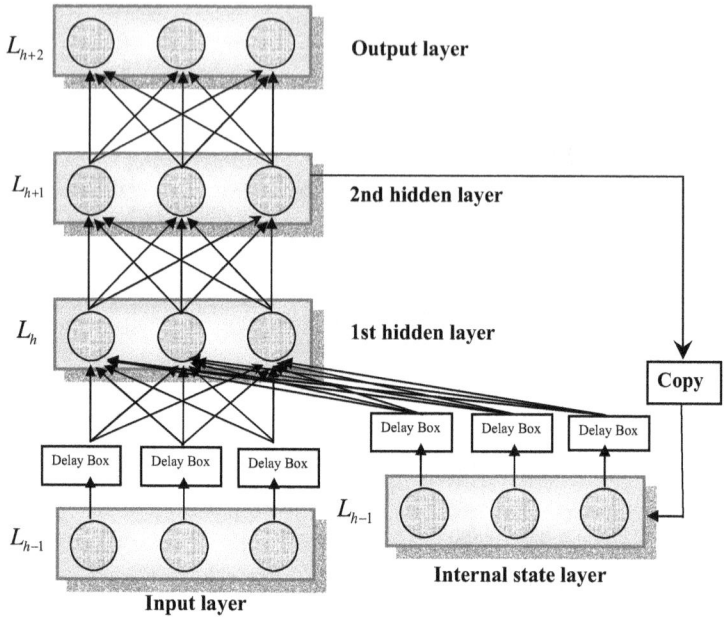

L_{h+2} Output layer

L_{h+1} 2nd hidden layer

L_h 1st hidden layer

Copy

Delay Box   Delay Box   Delay Box

Delay Box   Delay Box   Delay Box

L_{h-1}

L_{h-1}

Internal state layer

Input layer

Source: Time-delay recurrent neural network for temporal correlation and prediction. (Kim, 1998)

Note: L_{h+i} represents the layer $h + i$.

Figure 5. The architecture of the TDRNN

3.1.4. Radial basis function neural network (RBFNN)

We employ the RBFNN model to estimate the optimal components for ACU since its possess outstanding ability to seek for certainty factors and compare the testing result with the BPN model. (Donald and Krzysztof 1995) The RBF network was first presented by Broomhead and Lowe (1988) in the design and adapt of basic neural network in 1988. To constitute the RBF model was generally exert hybrid learning method. Specifically, it combined unsupervised and supervised learning rules. It utilizes unsupervised learning to select cluster center and to determine initial value. Finally, we adjusted the connection weight for nodes of hidden layer based on supervised learning regulation. (Chang and Huang, 2003; Su and Chang 2004)

As in the architecture of BPN, the RBF model was consisted by three layers. (Broomhead and Lowe 1988; Moody and Darken 1989) In the first input layer, the data was imported into each nodes of single hidden layer. Next, to calculate the distance from its own center to the input value and to determine the optimal number of cluster center in second layer, Donald (1995) indicated that the euclidean norm is the most widely regulation for calculating distance. The Euclidean regulation was shown as equation (3.9). One of major features for RBF neural network is to establish many of radial basis functions via curve fitting to find out mapping relationship between input and output

25

values. The *Gaussian function* is the most widely used in RBF neural network. (Donald and Krzysztof 1995; Chang and Huang, 2003) The graphical demonstration of an RBFNN model was shown in Figure 6.

$$v_i = \sqrt{\sum_{j=1}^{k} \left(x_j - c_{ji}\right)^2}, \qquad (3.9)$$

where value c demonstrates the center of cluster for each nodes of hidden layer. The x means input vector. The vector v represents array of length between input nodes and each hidden layer's cluster center. Then, the radial basis function which is mathematical formulation of the Gaussian functions can be written as follow:

$$R\left(\|x - c\|\right) = \exp\left(-\frac{\|x - c\|^2}{2\sigma^2}\right), \qquad (3.10)$$

where the $\|x - c_j\|$ denotes euclidean distance between x and c_j.

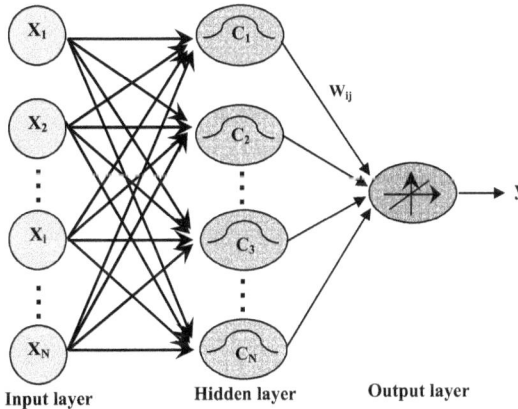

Figure 6. The architecture for the RBFNN model

3.1.5. Adaptive network-based fuzzy inference system (ANFIS)

In regard to obtain the efficient factors for exchange rate study, Wu and Goo (2005) exert ANFIS (adaptive-network-based fuzzy inference system) to analyze the short-term change in Taiwanese dollar. The ANFIS model was compromised of two input nodes, four fuzzy rules from Takagi and Sugeno (1985) establishment, and one output. In ANFIS manipulating process, the total sample is 300 daily information from the first quarter of 2004 to March 2005. The input vectors included Taiwan stock index (TSI), the foreign direct investment (FDI), the Japanese Yen/US$, Korean Won/US$, Euro/US$ and the lagged NT$/US$ exchange rate. The final results show that all of variables are important for testing the change in the short-term NT$/US$.

26

In this part, we utilize the ANFIS model to analyze source of contagion effect in ten Asian currencies. We take advantages of ANFIS model in terms of its shorter convergence time and superior training effect than the ANN model. (Nayak et al., 2004). The purpose is to estimate the relevant influence in financial linkage, trade linkage and macroeconomic similarity for each sample country. We follow the trade competition computation from Glick and Rose (1999) to generate the trade linkage indicator. The trade linkage equation can be shown as follow:

$$Trade_i \equiv \sum \left\{ \left[(x_{0k} + x_{ik}) / (x_{0.} + x_{i.}) \right] \cdot \left[1 - \left| (x_{ik} - x_{0k}) / (x_{ik} + x_{0k}) \right| \right] \right\}, \tag{3.11}$$

where 0 means the "first victim" country, x_{ik} indicates aggregate bilateral exports from country i to country k and $x_{i.}$ represents aggregate bilateral exports from country $i \cdot$. In light of the finance competition for bank funds, we utilize similar indicator of financial competition from Van Rijckeghem and Weder (2001). They denote estimation variable for financial linkage as follow:

$$Financial_i \equiv (b_{0c} + b_{ic}) / (b_0 + b_i) \left[1 - \left| ((b_{0c} / b_0) - (b_{ic} / b_i)) ((b_{0c} / b_0) + (b_{ic} / b_i)) \right| \right], \tag{3.12}$$

where 0 means the "first victim" country, c represents the common lender, and b_{ic} stands for bank loan from country c to country i. Finally, the macroeconomic fundamental extracted from relevant paper have explained the incidence of currency crises. The relevant variables used in this study were: (a) the ratio of M2 to international reserves: (b) the current account balance as a percent of GDP: (c) the ratio of government budget deficit (surplus) to GDP. (d) the discount rate; (e) the ratio of short-term debt to reserves. (Van Rijckeghem and Weder, 2001)

3.1.5.1. Fuzzy inference system (FIS)

When it comes to adaptive network-based fuzzy inference system, this model is the property of a Neuro-Fuzzy computing technique. (Jang, 1993; Zhang and Huang, 2003) The Fuzzy Inference System (FIS) was developed from fuzzy logic. (Zadeh, 1973) This technique could construct mapping relation between input and output values. Based on input membership functions (MFs) to map input feature, it could transfer the input value into a membership value between 0 and 1. Then the input MFs could convert into the output MFs through fuzzy rules. As a result, a single output value was been created. Figure 7. shows a architecture of an FIS which was composed of three main parts. A database provides the MFs and relative parameters to the fuzzy rules and fuzzy sets; a rule base sort of knowledge and selection for fuzzy rules and an inference process combines above function to map an output.

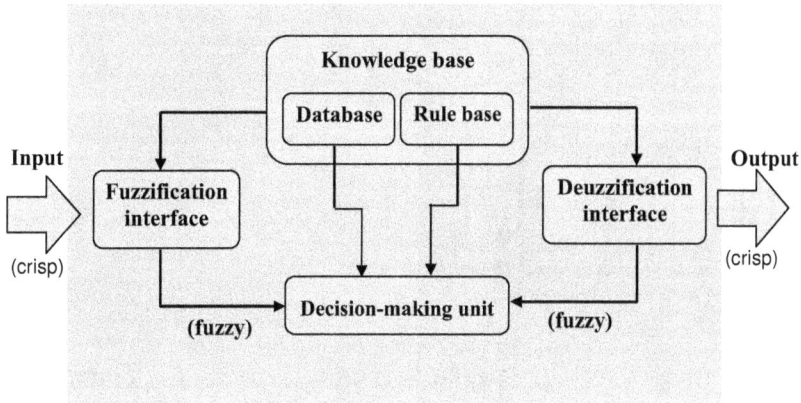

Source: Adaptive-Network-Based Fuzzy Inference System. (Jang Jyh-Shing, 1993)

Figure 7. Fuzzy inference system

3.1.5.2. The architecture of the ANFIS

The adaptive neuro fuzzy inference system (ANFIS) was presented by Jang (1993). It belongs to feed-forward neural network with supervised learning capability which possesses the same feature with MLP model. The ANFIS combines two algorithm's characteristics including fuzzy inference system and neural network. In other words, the architecture of the ANFIS is to enhance fuzzy logic on artificial neural network. The purposes are to progress treatment capability in connection with uncertainty and imprecisely of system forecasting and equipped with organization learning ability simultaneously. (Jang, 1993) A hybrid learning rule combined the gradient steepest method and the least squares estimate (LSE) to revise the parameters. Besides, by appling the first-order Sugeno FIS yields rule bases. (Takagi and Sugeno, 1985) For simplicity, we set up two if-then rules to further explain the concept of Sugeno fuzzy rule.

Rule 1: If X is A_1 and Y is B_1, then

$$f_1 = p_1\chi + q_1 y + \gamma_1,$$

Rule 2: If X is A_2 and Y is B_2, then

$$f_2 = p_2\chi + q_2 y + \gamma_2, \tag{3.13}$$

where A_i and B_i represent the membership functions (MFs) for inputs x and y, and p_i, q_i, γ_i represent the parameters of the output function. Figure 8 demonstrates how the fuzzy logic to generate an output value f from a given input vector. The output f also indicates the weighted average of each rule's output.

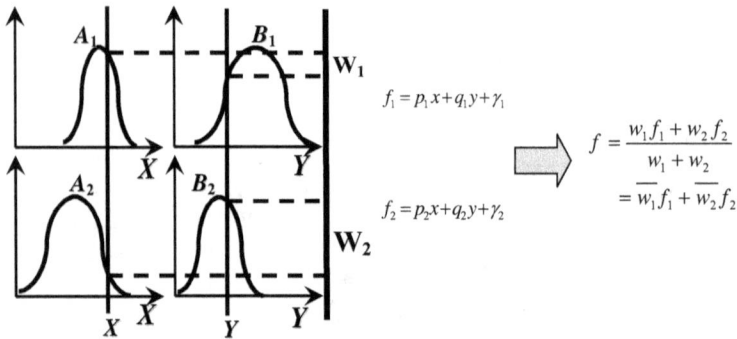

$f_1 = p_1 x + q_1 y + \gamma_1$

$f = \dfrac{w_1 f_1 + w_2 f_2}{w_1 + w_2}$

$= \overline{w}_1 f_1 + \overline{w}_2 f_2$

$f_2 = p_2 x + q_2 y + \gamma_2$

Source: Adaptive-Network-Based Fuzzy Inference System. (Jang Jyh-Shing, 1993)

Figure 8. First-order Sugeno fuzzy model

The architecture of the ANFIS contains totally five layers. Each layer's function and structure was shown as follows. (Jang, 1993; Jang and Sun, 1995; Jang, 1997; and Wu and Goo, 2005)

Layer 1: Input nodes

In first layer, the main function is to map the input nodes into fuzzy sets so as to enhance the treatment capability of this model. For instance, Figure 9 shows variable X was decomposed into two fuzzy sets A_1 and A_2, and each node i should be exhibited by a membership function. In light of the precise illustration and outstanding performance for the bell-shaped functions, we select the *bell shaped function* to be the MFs in this study. (Mascioli and Martinelli, 1997; Wu and Goo, 2005)

$$O_{1,ji} = \mu_j(\chi_i) = \frac{1}{1 + \left| \dfrac{\chi_i - c_{ji}}{a_{ji}} \right|^{2b_{ji}}}, \text{ for } \quad i = 1,2,...,N; j = 1,2...,M_j. \qquad (3.14)$$

where parameters $\{a_i, b_i, c_i\}$ represent set of MFs in the fuzzy if-then rules: c_i indicates the middle value of the MF; a_i means the half width; and b_i is a parameter to controls the slope at the crossover points. $\mu_j(\chi_i)$ represents input nodes i in set of membership function j.

Layer 2: rule nodes

Next step is to coordinate each fuzzy set of input node with rules of fuzzy logic computation. A_i and B_j indicated that the linguistic symbols characterized by the bell shape of the membership function. In this paper, we utilized the T-norm computing method to implement the fuzzy calculation.

$$O_2, k = Wk = uA_i(\chi) \times uB_j(y), \quad k = 1,....,k. \qquad (3.15)$$

where O_2, k represents the outcomes from layer 1.

29

Layer 3: normalization nodes

The k means the normalization output from previous layer. More precisely, we use i_{th} rule node's output divided by all rules node's output. As a result, the output values show in the range between 0 and 1. Noted that $\overline{w_k}$ means the outcome of normalizing.

$$O_3,k = \overline{w_k} = \frac{w_k}{\sum\limits_{k=1}^{k} w_k},$$
(3.16)

Layer 4: consequent nodes

In this layer, we employ the node's output from previous layer to multiply the first-order Sugeno fuzzy mode.

$$O_4,k = \overline{w_k} f_k = \overline{w_k}(p_i x + q_i y + \gamma_i),$$
(3.17)

where $\{p_i, q_i, \gamma_i\}$ determines the relative coefficients based on the consequent of the first-order Sugeno fuzzy model.

Layer 5: output nodes

We manipulate one output node in this model, and utilize technique of defuzzificaton inference to convert the fuzzy outcome into a crisp value. We sum all previous layer nodes' output as equation 3.16.

$$O_5,_1 = \sum\limits_{k=1}^{k} \overline{w_k} f_k = \frac{\sum\limits_{k=1}^{k} w_k f_k}{\sum\limits_{k=1}^{k} w_k},$$
(3.18)

where $\sum\limits_{k=1}^{k} \overline{w_k} f_k$ represents overall output after using $\overline{w_k}$ output value to multiply the first-order Sugeno fuzzy model.

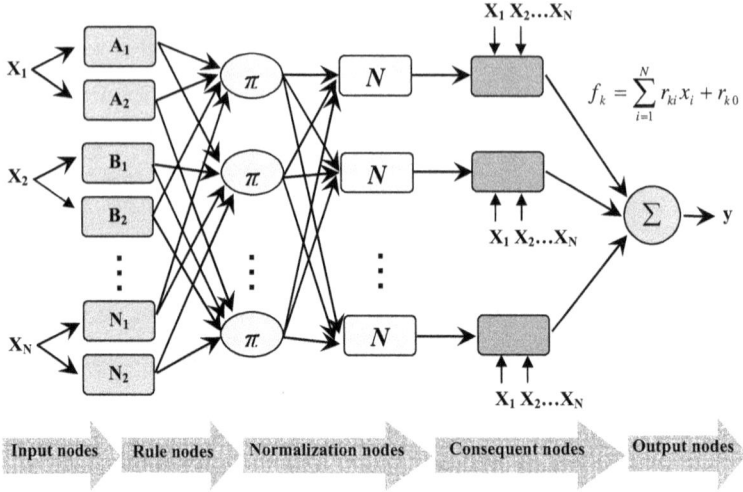

$$f_k = \sum_{i=1}^{N} r_{ki} x_i + r_{k0}$$

Figure 9. The ANFIS architecture for N_{th} **input nodes and one output node**

3.2. General autoregressive conditional heteroscedasticity model (GARCH)

In this section, GARCH approach was compared with artificial neural network. The ARCH model was briefly introduced first, because the GARCH model was evolved from the ARCH model.

3.2.1. Autoregressive conditional heterocedasticity (ARCH)

ARCH model was proposed by Engle (1982). To solve unreasonable assumption in fixed conditional heterocedasticity, Engle revises and adjusts the new movement process through time in terms of conditional heterocedasticity. Equation 3.17 shows ARCH model containing disturbance term which influenced by previous q periods:

$$Y_t = X_t b + \varepsilon_t,$$
$$Y_t \,|\psi_{t-1} \sim N(X_t b, h_t),$$
$$\varepsilon_t = Y_t - X_t b, \tag{3.19}$$
$$h_t = h(\varepsilon_{t-1}, \varepsilon_{t-2}, ..., \varepsilon_{t-q}; \alpha)$$
$$= h_t(\psi_{t-1}; \alpha).$$

where X_t is a exogenous variable; ψ_{t-1} indicates all of the available information sets including realized disturbance term at the past; h_t represents the conditional heterocedasticity function; and $N(X_t b, h_t)$ shows distribution parameters in regard to mean $(X_t b)$ and variance (h_t).

3.2.2. General Autoregressive Conditional Heteroscedasticity Model; GARCH

When it comes to the GARCH model, Engle (1982) first represents Autoregressive Conditional

Heterocedasticity model (ARCH) to analyze inconsistent variance condition. Based on Engle's model, Bollersler (1986) further extend the ARCH model. He starts to put self-repressor into equation for developing model, called GRACH model. Reviewing some papers related forecasting of exchange rate by using GRACH (1, 1) model. Caporale and Doroodian (1994), Hwang (1998), Chen (1999) and Yuko (2004) estimated cross-rate volatility influence process via the GRACH family model. For instance, Caporale and Doroodian conducted analysis of real exchange volatility between US dollar and Canadian dollar. They utilized the GARCH model to estimate variable influence to exchange rate under nonstationary state. It proved that uncertainty of exchange rate could exhibit significantly negative influence to trade flow based on GARCH model. Hwang employs daily information of five main countries currency (such as German, England, French, Swiss, and Japan) against US dollars. The purpose is to estimate five countries' currency rate movement to find out fitness model for exchange rate volatility. She also takes the financial crisis to be the dummy variable into the empirical models. Based on the results from GARCH (1, 1), she proves that the coefficient of dummy variable exhibits significant results that increase the volatility of five currencies. Chen compares the currency impact of Japanese Yen and Germany Mark by Asia Financial Crisis. As the result, the conditional heterocedasticity of Japanese yen exhibits significant in pre- and post- crisis. This result indicates that the impact of Japanese yen is greater than that of Germany mark.

Although the simple GARCH model would estimate the volatility of exchange rate and it allows for a longer memory in the conditional variance process than ARCH model. However, the GARCH (1, 1) model existed the probability of non-convergent solution. (Hu and Christos, 1999). In light of this perspective, this study utilities the ANN models because of its low constraint for assumption. For comparison, the GRACH (1, 1) model was applied to compare with the artificial neural network in terms of forecasting performance in regard to creating Asian currency unit.

Bollerslev (1986) altered the ARCH model by adding a lagged conditional heteroscedasticity h_{t-j} to overcome overly complex parameters manipulation. The architecture of equation displays as following.

$$Y_t = X_t b + \varepsilon_t,$$
$$Y_t | \psi_{t-1} \sim N(X_t b, h_t),$$
$$\varepsilon_t | \psi_{t-1} \sim N(0, h_t),$$
$$\varepsilon_t = Y_t - X_t b, \qquad \qquad \text{(3.20)}$$
$$h_t = \alpha_0 + \alpha_1 \varepsilon_{t-1}^2 + \ldots + \beta_1 h_{t-1} + \ldots + \beta_p h_{t-p}$$
$$= \alpha_0 + \sum_{i=1}^{q} \alpha_i \varepsilon_{t-i}^2 + \sum_{j=1}^{p} \beta_j h_{t-j}$$
$$= \alpha_0 + A(L)\varepsilon_t^2 + B(L)h_t .$$

where $\quad A(L) = 1 + \alpha_1 L + ... + \alpha_q L^q$,

$\quad\quad\quad B(L) = 1 + \beta_1 L + ... + \beta_p L^p \cdot$

The L represents lag operator and other relative information shown as below.

$p \geq 0; q \geq 0,$

$\alpha_0 > 0; \alpha_i \geq 0; i = 1...q,$

$\beta_j \geq 0, j = 1...p \cdot$

Since the conditional heteroscedasticity equipped with properties of previous disturbance square and lagged conditional variance, the conditional variance models could be more flexible. In this paper, we apply the GARCH (1, 1) because of its simplicity and stability. Hwang (1998) and West and Cho (1995) revealed that GARCH models can provide a better forecasting performance of exchange rate prediction.

3.3. Testing and verify criteria

In this study, we utilize RMSE and MSE and NMSE to be the major principles for evaluating our testing model analysis results.

3.3.1. Root Mean-Square Error (RMSE)

In regard to the convergence testing for our empirical models, the RMSE could provide a notable research performance for test. We use this criterion to estimate the error convergence content. The smallest value of RMSE means this model represent best forecasting power for output variable. The equation was shown as follow: (Qi and Zhang 2001; Yeh 2002)

$$RMSE = \frac{\sqrt{\sum_{i}^{M}\sum_{j}^{N}\left(A_j^i - D_j^i\right)^2}}{M \cdot N}, \tag{3.21}$$

where A_j^i represents actual output value from j output layer of example i,

$\quad\quad\quad D_j^i$ represents desired output value from j output layer of example i,

$\quad\quad\quad M$ represents the number of exemplifications,

$\quad\quad\quad N$ represents the number of nodes for output layer.

3.3.2. Mean-Square Error (MSE)

This index is a measure of the dispersed degree between desired value and actual value. The smaller value of MSE represents the smaller dispersed degree. In other words, the model result is better. The equation was shown as follow:(Chang 2004)

$$MSE = \frac{\sum_{i}^{M}\sum_{j}^{N}\left(A_j^i - D_j^i\right)^2}{M \cdot N}, \tag{3.22}$$

where A_j^i represents actual output value from j output layer of example i,

D^i_j represents desired output value from j output layer of example i,

M represents the number of exemplifications,

N represents the number of nodes for output layer.

3.3.3. Normalized mean-square error (NMSE)

We employ this index to estimate prediction performance of the neural networks. When the NMSE shows zero which indicates perfect forecasting for this network and an NMSE of unity represents this prediction performance is inferior to a constant predictor at $E[x(t)]$. The definition of NMSE was shown as the following: (Yu, Wang and Lai 2005)

$$NMSE = \frac{E\left[x(t) - \hat{x}(t)^2\right]}{E\left[(x(t) - E[x(t)])^2\right]},$$
(3.23)

where $x(t)$ denotes the original value and $\hat{x}(t)$ means the prediction value from network.

3.4. The computation approach of ACU

This study utilizes the mechanism of current basket in Euro to constitute Asian Currency Unit. The central exchange rate was consisted by currency exchange rate of ten Asia countries which included Taiwan, Japan, South Korea, Hong Kong, Malaysia, Singapore, Thailand, Philippine, Indonesia and Mainland against U.S. Dollars. In regard to selecting macroeconomic variables, central exchange rate of ACU was composed of weights of Export Volume, Net Reverse and GDP per Capita. The detail calculation steps were shown in Figure 10. Due to the fact that the volatility in political and economic issues is more serious than members of EU, under such circumstance, the period of realigning exchange rate of ACU is determined in three year one time[19]. The period covers from March 2, 1992 to June 30, 2005. We have showed the tendency chart in terms of ACU against U.S. Dollars for past thirteen years. We collect the data from AERMOS database, Taiwan Economic Journal (TEJ) and Asian Development Bank (Key Indicators, 2005). (Appendix)

---

[19] Chen, Wang and Lin, 2001; Chen 2001; Chen and Hsieh, 2004; Chen and Hisao, 2004; Chen and Chen, 2006.

The steps of computing ACU	Computing Formulation: The unit of each country's current basket =
	$$\left(\dfrac{\text{each country's export volume}}{\text{summation of each country's export volume}} \right.$$ $$+$$ $$\dfrac{\text{each country's net reverse}}{\text{summation of each country's net reverse}}$$ $$+$$ $$\dfrac{\text{each country's GDP per capita}}{\text{summation of each country's GDP per capita}}$$ $$\times$$ $$\text{The exchange rate against US dollars}$$ $$\times$$ $$\left. \text{SDR} \right)$$
Step 1.	Gathering the data of Export Volume, Net Reserve and GDP per Capita on five base periods in march 1992, march 1995, march 1998, march 2001 and march 2004. The research sample retrieves from nine currencies in ten countries.
Step 2.	Computing average weight ratio of above three variables in five base periods respectively.
Step 3.	Calculating SDR ratio when weight against USD.
Step 4.	Computing each country's weight on respective variables in five base times.
Step 5.	Figure out each country's unit in current basket, each country's value of Export Volume, Net Reserve and GDP per Capita multiply each variable's weight. Consequently, the percent of summation weight multiply exchange rate against USD and multiply SDR. Consequently, based on the unit in current basket, we can further calculate the weight of each base period.
Step 6.	Using each country's unit in current basket to multiply each country's cross exchange rate could receive individual value in ACU.
Step 7.	Converting each currency's value in ACU to USD so as to generating central rate of ACU.

Source: Organized by the Author.

Figure 10. The computation approach of ACU

Chapter 4. Empirical results

4.1. Forecasting performance for ACU

In first part, we compare the forecasting capability in terms of central rate of ACU between artificial neural networks and GARCH (1, 1). With regard to the ANN models, we further select three brilliant ANN models to conduct prediction of central rate of ACU including BPN, RNN, and TDRNN. To select the training and testing sets is very important step. Different period selections may result in a poor forecasting performance mainly because some unexpected variance may happen in the time series. In order not to miss any available information for the forecasting process of ANN model, we manipulate six types of training data and testing data via randomly selected proportion[20]. (Andreou et al, 2002) In a wake of implementing different iteration exanimation (i.e. 1000, 10000, 100000) for each ANN models, based on the testing results of RMSE and NMSE, the best epoch number is 100,000 so that we choose it to be model's standard parameter for maximum epochs.

In analyzing each forecasting performance, the RMSE and NMSE are main criteria for evaluating the results. The detail parameter setting and estimating outcomes for ANN's were shown in Table 3.

---

[20] i.e. 80% training data and 20% testing data (I); 75% training data and 25% testing data (II); 70% training data and 30% testing data (III); 60% training testing and 40% testing data (IV); 55% training data and 45% testing data (V); 50% training data and 50% testing data (VI).

Table 3 ANN's testing results for six types of training and testing data

Types	Parameters Setting	Back-Propagation Neural Network (BPN)	Recurrent Neural Network (RNN)	Time-Lag Recurrent Neural Network (TDRNN)
	Hidden Nodes	10	10	10
	Transfer Function	Sigmoid	Sigmoid	Sigmoid
	Learning Rate	0.7	0.7	0.7
	Maximum Epochs	100,000	100,000	100,000
	Testing Data	144	144	144
	MSE	3.97E-06	1.22E-04	3.36E-05
I	NMSE	1.39E-04	4.26E-03	1.17E-03
	R-Square	0.9998	0.9972	0.9992
	Testing Data	181	181	181
	MSE	4.78E-06	2.74E-04	1.52E-05
II	NMSE	1.69E-04	9.73E-03	5.38E-04
	R-Square	0.9998	0.9932	0.9996
	Testing Data	217	217	217
	MSE	6.05E-06	1.22E-04	2.17E-05
III	NMSE	2.46E-04	4.26E-03	8.82E-03
	R-Square	0.9999	0.9972	0.9993
	Testing Data	289	289	289
	MSE	1.03E-05	2.38E-04	1.38E-05
IV	NMSE	4.42E-04	1.01E-02	5.93E-03
	R-Square	0.9998	0.9934	0.9995
	Testing Data	325	325	325
	MSE	2.79E-05	4.09E-04	1.56E-05
V	NMSE	1.34E-03	1.62E-02	6.33E-03
	R-Square	0.9997	0.9909	0.9995
	Testing Data	362	362	362
	MSE	2.67E-05	2.62E-04	1.97E-05
VI	NMSE	9.91E-04	9.67E-03	7.26E-04
	R-Square	0.9998	0.9962	0.9995

According to empirical results from three ANN models, BPN model exhibits better performance ability for testing exchange rate of ACU at 20%, 25%, 30%, and 40% testing data. The values of MSE at above four segment periods are all lower than others. There are 3.97E-06, 4.78E-06, 6.05E-06 and 1.03E-05, respectively. On the other hand, TDRNN model indicates better performance for estimating exchange rate of ACU which contains 45% and 50% testing data. The values of MSE are 1.56E-05 and 1.97E-05, respectively. These values were smaller than other ANN models. However, RNN model didn't show outstanding performance regarding to exchange rate forecasting of ACU regarding to its poor performance in MSE and NMSE. We have manipulated forecasting chart for three ANN models in six different division cases which compare with actual value of ACU. The Figures 11-16 was shown as following. We could check each value of desired outputs for BPN, TDRNN, and RNN if it closes to the actual value of ACU exchange rate. For instance, the BPN has the most proximate outcomes with the actual value of ACU in the Figure 11.

Table 4 shows the testing result of the best ANN model in each different forecasting period and compare it with GARCH (1, 1) in terms of RMSE. Incontrovertibly, the ANN models have superior forecasting capability to the GARCH (1, 1) whether comparing with BPN or TDRNN model. For instance, in the case of 20% testing set, the value of RMSE for BPN is 0.0019 which extreme lower than GARCH (1, 1) at value of 1.3903. Moreover, we take another extreme example for 50% testing data. The result shows that the value of RMSE for TDRNN is 0.0044. Again, it's much lower than GARCH (1, 1) at value of 1.3685.

Table 4   The forecasting result of ACU based on the best ANN models when weight against the GARCH (1, 1)

	Back-Propagation neural network (BPN)	GARCH (1, 1)
20% testing data (144)	**RMSE (0.0019)	RMSE (1.3903)
25% testing data (181)	**RMSE (0.0022)	RMSE (1.3711)
30% testing data (217)	**RMSE (0.0025)	RMSE (1.3520)
40% testing data (289)	**RMSE (0.0032)	RMSE (1.3521)
	Time-Lag Recurrent Neural Network (TRNN)	**GARCH (1, 1)**
45% testing data (325)	**RMSE (0.0039)	RMSE (1.3646)
50% testing data (362)	**RMSE (0.0044)	RMSE (1.3685)

Note: 1. **indicates better performance consequence based on the testing criteria of RMSE.
2. the numbers of weekly information are illustrated in the parentheses.

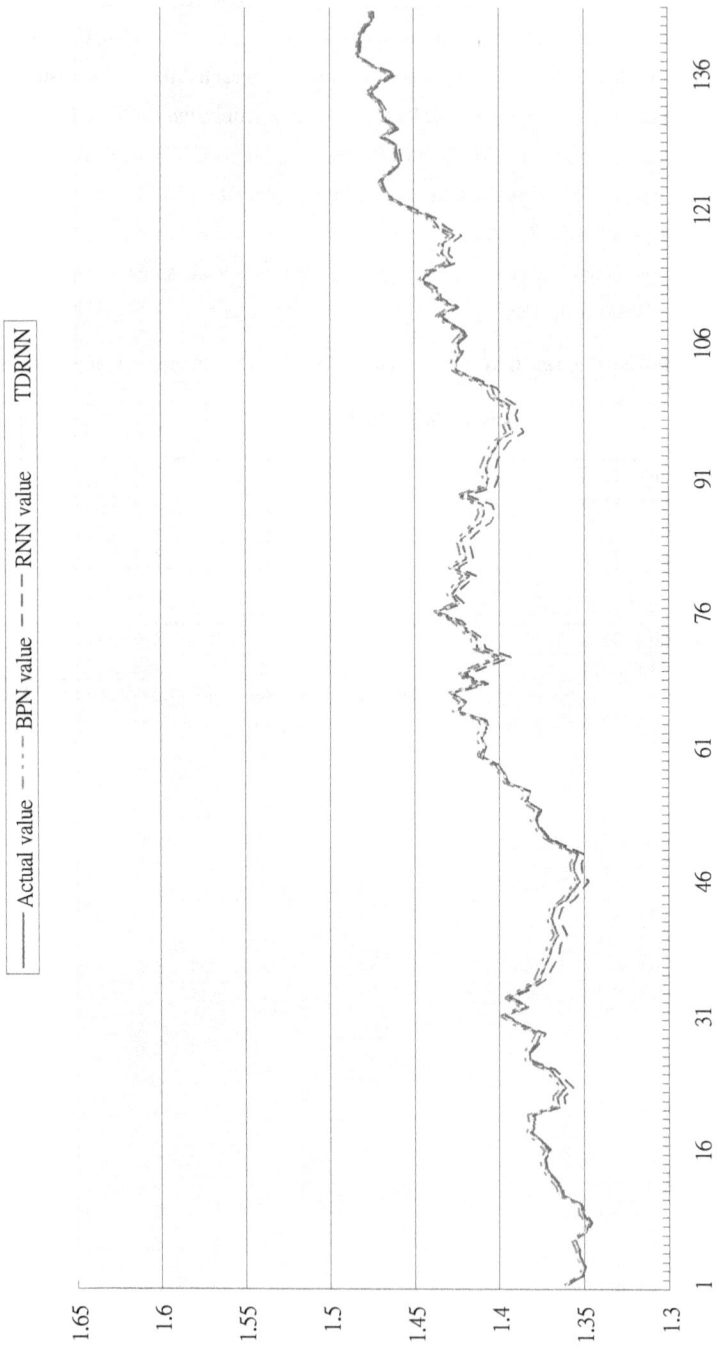

Figure 11. ANN's forecasting chart for 80% training, 20% testing

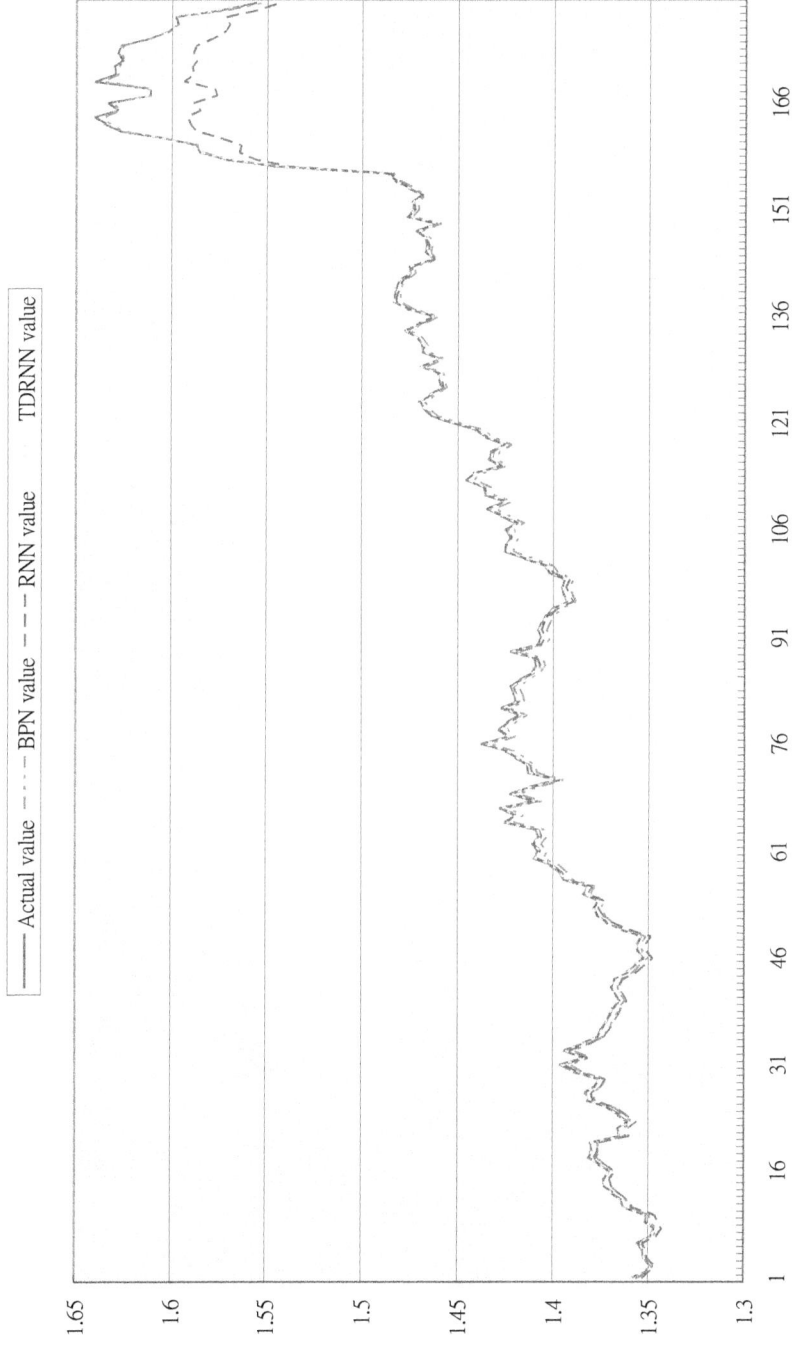

Figure 12. ANN's forecasting chart for 75% training, 25% testing

40

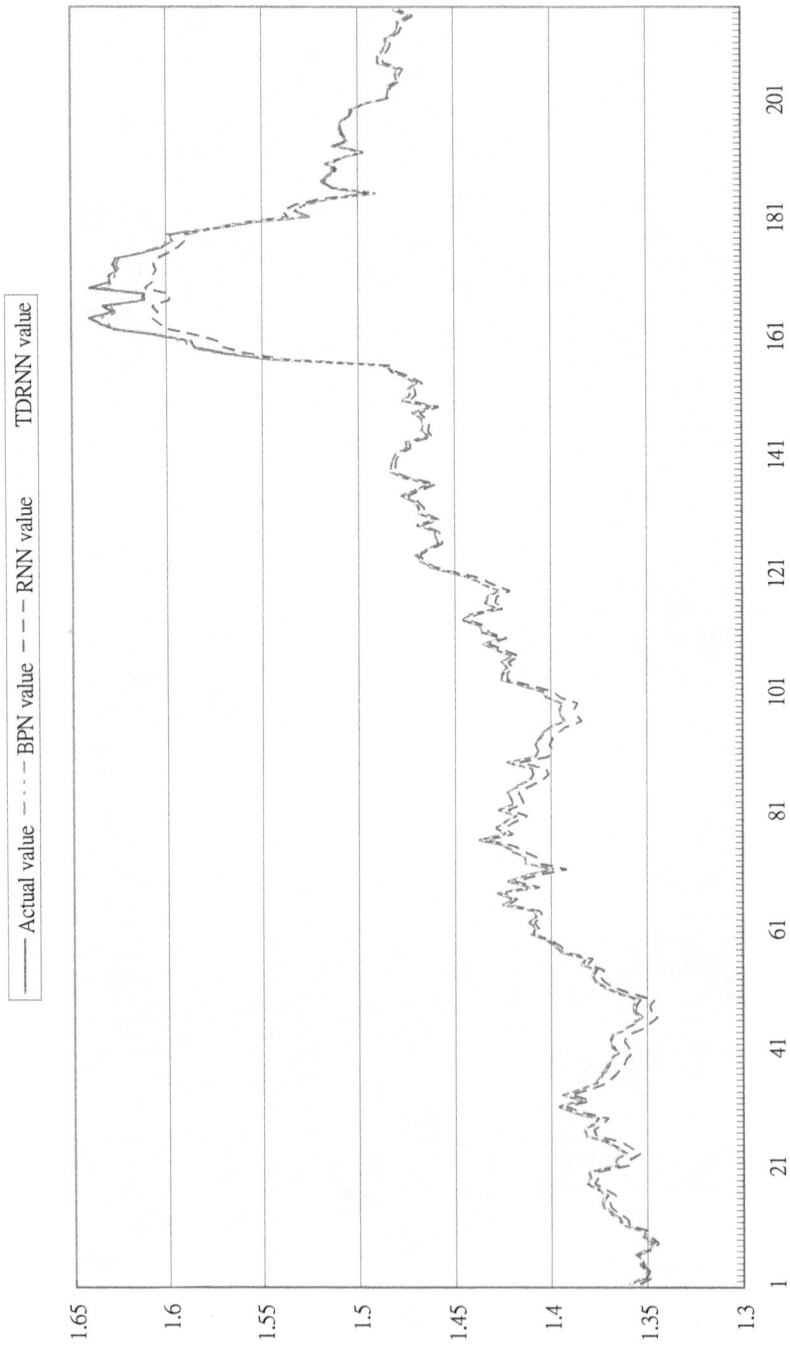

Legend: —— Actual value — · · — BPN value — — — RNN value TDRNN value

Figure 13. ANN's forecasting chart for 70% training, 30% testing

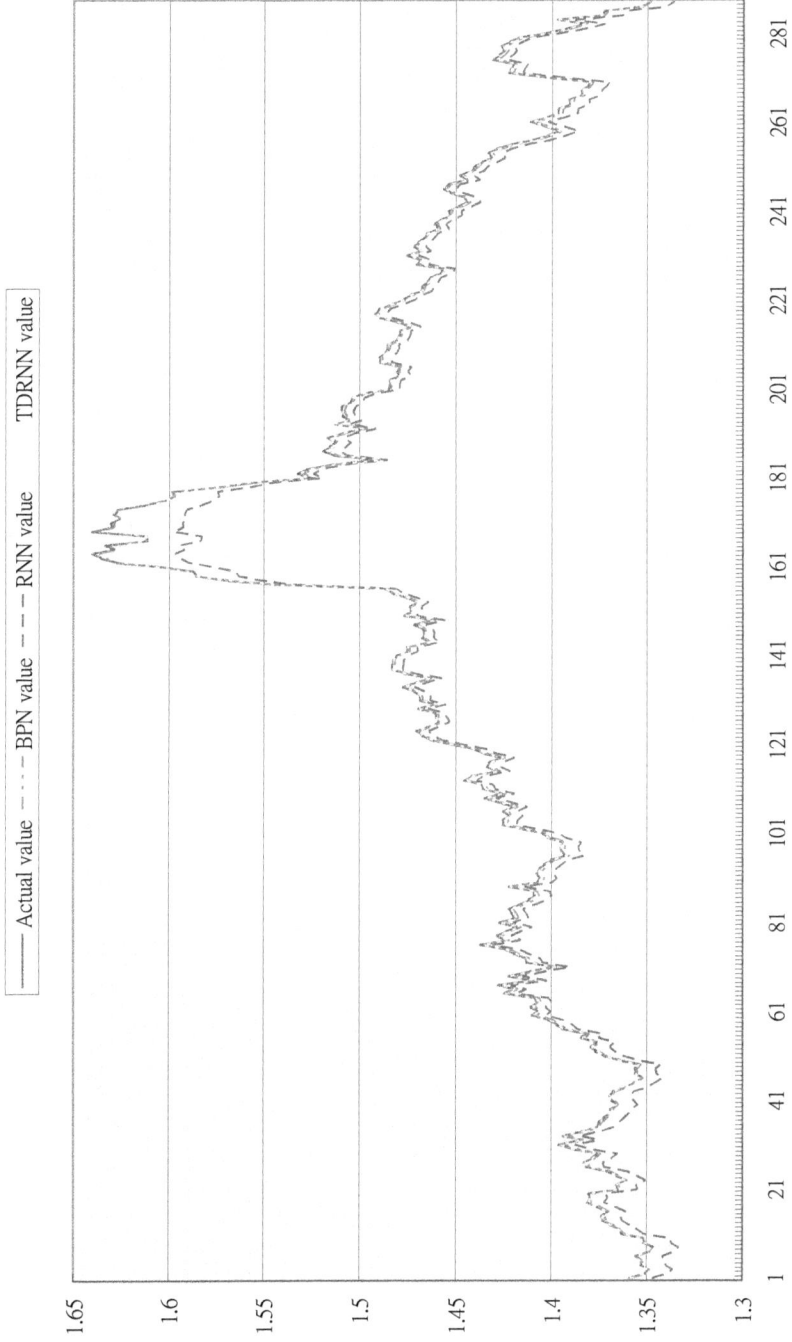

Figure 14. ANN's forecasting chart for 60% training, 40% testing

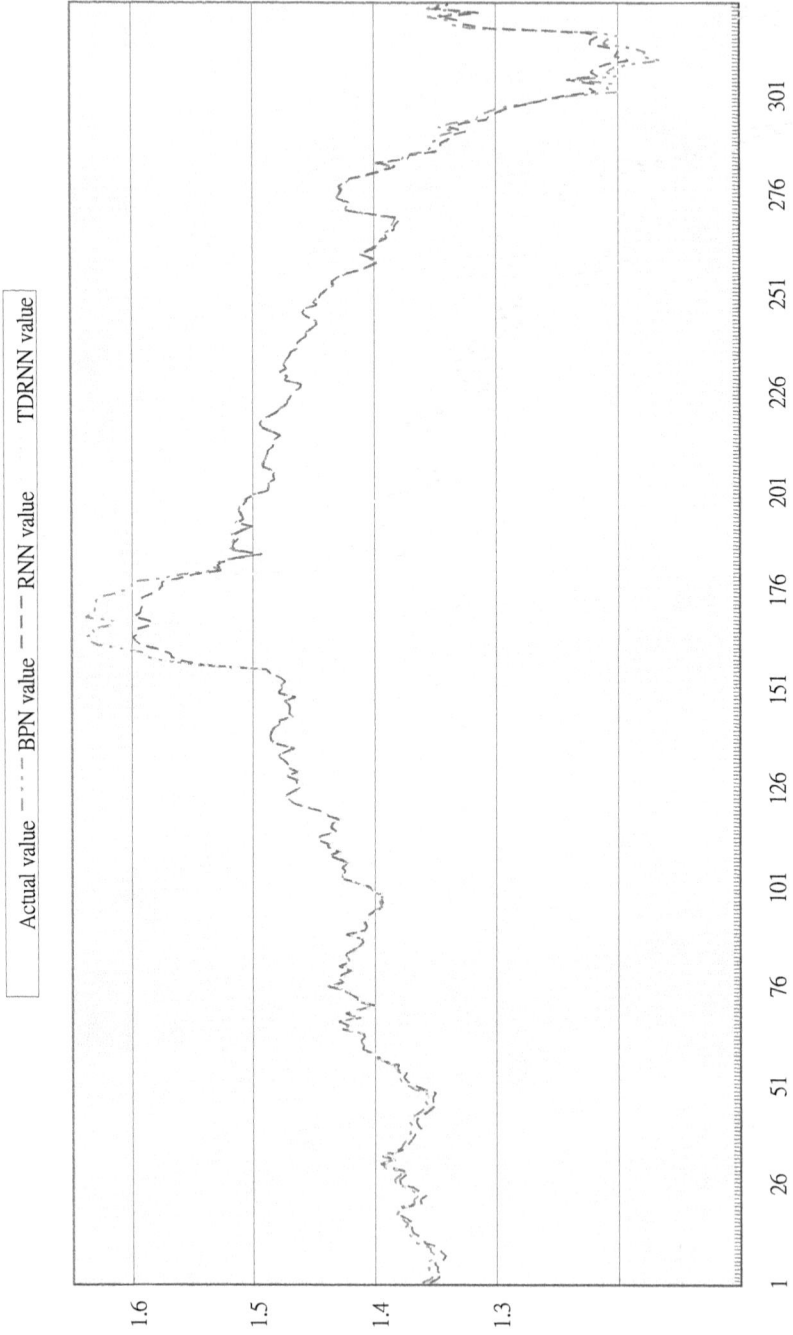

Actual value — · · — BPN value — — RNN value   TDRNN value

Figure 15. ANN's forecasting chart for 55% training, 45% testing

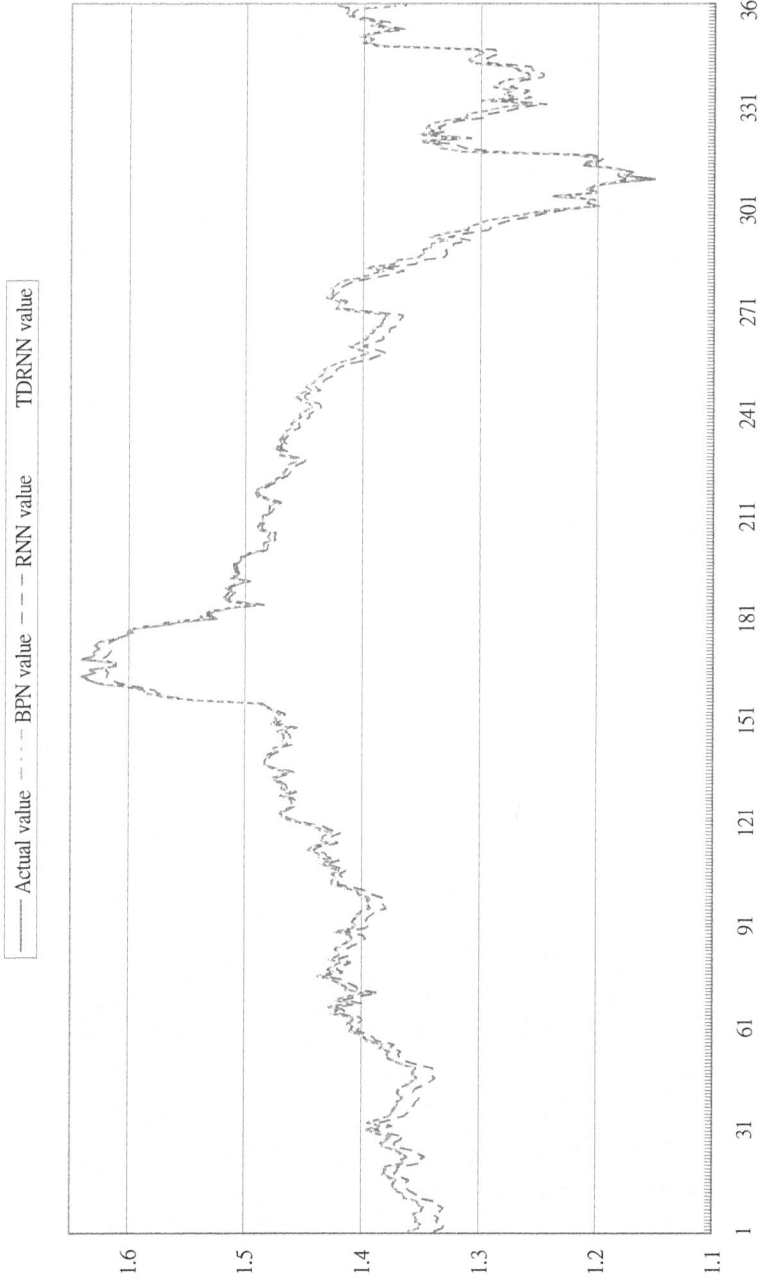

Figure 16. ANN's forecasting chart for 50% training, 50% testing

4.2. The testing results of optimal components

We set up eight different models for each country estimate optimal components analysis for ACU. Each country's central value of ACU was utilized to be the output value for the ANN models. The detail information for those setting models was shown as following:

- Model 1: $INX_{ij} + RE_{ij} + Y_{ij}$,
- Model 2: $INX_{ij} + RE_{ij} + Y_{ij} + FDI/G_{ij}$,
- Model 3: $INX_{ij} + RE_{ij} + Y_{ij} + Ed/G_{ij}$,
- Model 4: $INX_{ij} + RE_{ij} + Y_{ij} + B/G_{ij}$,
- Model 5: $INX_{ij} + RE_{ij} + Y_{ij} + FDI/G_{ij} + Ed/G_{ij}$,
- Model 6: $INX_{ij} + RE_{ij} + Y_{ij} + FDI/G_{ij} + B/G_{ij}$,
- Model 7: $INX_{ij} + RE_{ij} + Y_{ij} + Ed/G_{ij} + B/G_{ij}$,
- Model 8: $INX_{ij} + RE_{ij} + Y_{ij} + FDI/G_{ij} + Ed/G_{ij} + B/G_{ij}$,

where   INX : export volume ,

RE : international reverse ,

Y : GDP per capita ,

FDI/G : the ratio of foreign direct investment to GDP ,

ED/G : the ratio of external debt to GDP ,

B/G : the ratio of bank's claim on private sector to GDP ·

4.2.1. Parameters setting for the ANN models

In this study, our testing sample was determined from first quarter 1992 to third quarter 2005. Except for original components[21] (i.e. export volume, net reserve and GDP per capita), we further add other three macroeconomic variables (such as the ratio of foreign direct investment to GDP, the ratio of external debt to GDP and the ratio of bank's claim on private sector to GDP) based on the report of releasing reference weights of flexible Renminbi from the People's Bank of China in July 2005. With regard to obtain the best fit model for testing the optimal components of Asian currency unit, we pre-examine parameters setting based on the BPN model for each country. At the very beginning, to determine the best number of hidden nodes is first step, then we further discuss how many hidden layers that suit for the country model. Consequently, we confirm the optimal maximum epoch and final term by estimating the effect of learning rate manipulation for each testing model.

At the first parameter testing, we follow the threshold setting of the NeuroSolutions to manipulate the learning rate at 0.7 and only discuss on the one hidden layer situation. The maximum epochs is determining in 10,000 times. Under above setting, the BPN model could reflect

---

[21] Chen, Wang and Lin, 2001; Chen 2001; Chen and Hsieh, 2004; Chen and Hisao, 2004; Chen and Chen, 2006.

45

the variation of hidden nodes' change. In regard to the determine criteria, we decide the fittest nodes based on the value of MSE and NMSE which the smallest value represents the best explain power for the BPN model. The testing result for each country's fittest hidden nodes was shown as Table 5.

In the wake of conducting hidden numbers examination, we have extended our BPN model to test two and three hidden layer outcomes. Without any sense of doubtful, it can't enhance the explain ability and the testing performance through increase the hidden layer numbers. All of samples show that the best performance was one hidden layer. In convergence condition, we compare three learning epoch setting such as 1,000, 10,000 and 100,000 times. Again, we estimate the testing result by using MSE and NMSE value. The 100,000 epochs indicate well testing results in all country's models. Finally, there are four different learning rates to be discussed in this section. Each learning rate represents different convergence speed for models. If the learning rate is too small for the model, it will cause longer convergence time and larger epochs for ANNs model. Although to set up overly higher learning rate could accelerate the effectiveness of convergence, the output value will generate unstable oscillation. With this in mind, we should further test finest learning rate for each county. According to the testing results for learning rate, the most of countries exhibit the prime rates at 0.5. However, the prime learning rate for Hong Kong and China are 0.05. Furthermore, Singapore and Thailand are 0.1. (Chang and Huang, 2003)

Table 5 Synthesizing information for ANN model's parameter setting for BPN model.

Country	Hidden Nodes	Hidden Layer	Maximum Epochs	Learning Rate
Japan	15	1	100,000	0.5
Hong Kong	7	1	100,000	0.05
Indonesia	15	1	100,000	0.5
Korea	7	1	100,000	0.5
Malaysia	7	1	100,000	0.5
Philippines	13	1	100,000	0.5
Singapore	15	1	100,000	0.1
Thailand	9	1	100,000	0.1
China	5	1	100,000	0.05
Taiwan	3	1	100,000	0.05

Note: We employ basic model (1) to implement the parameter test for BPN model.

4.2.2. Testing result for BPN and RBFN models

In a wake of determining the ANN model's parameters based on basis pattern (model 1) estimation, next approach is to diagnose the testing performance for all of the ANN models which were established by different macroeconomic variables. The result shows a number of findings pertaining to the optimal components of ACU in our estimating samples. Table 6 represents the summary consequences for Japan's BPN and RBFNN exanimations. The model (8) in BPN exhibits the most prominent performance mainly because its outstanding performance in terms of MSE and NMSE, suggesting that the six macro-variables which contained in optimal components analysis have significant explanation in regard to Japan's central weights in ACU. Table 7 demonstrates the summary consequences for Indonesia's BPN and RBFNN examinations. The results of Indonesia's model are consistent with Japan's consequence. The model (8) in BPN exhibits the most prominent performance, suggesting that the six macro-variables which contained in modified components analysis have significant explanation in regard to Indonesia's central weights in ACU. Furthermore, Taiwan has the same empirical results with Japan and Indonesia. It also provides an evidence for Taiwan to revise its basket components of ACU. The empirical results for Taiwan show in Table 8. However, Table 9 shows the empirical results of Korea's BPN and RBFNN examinations. To indicate the opposed consequence with Japan as well as Indonesia, the model (5) in BPN shows the best performance and the best model in RBFNN for Korea is model (8). The empirical result in Table 10 shows that Malaysia has consistent outcomes for modified components in BPN and RBFNN model. Both models indicate model (8) is the best testing result. It's fully support that Malaysia should consider six macro-variables into its modified basket components.

According to our testing results for modified components in Philippines and Thailand which represent in Table 11 and Table 12, they have the same empirical results for BPN and RBFNN examinations. The best model for BPN is model (8) and model (6) is finest one for RBFNN.

47

Moreover, these two countries show quiet excellent value in BPN model in terms of MSE and NMSE. In other words, it indicates the lowest error when using all macro-variables to express the central weights of ACU for Philippines and Thailand. On the other hand, Singapore, China and Hong Kong exhibit different finest in BPN when weight against others countries. The detail information for Singapore and Hong Kong was shown in Table 13 and Table 14, respectively. We find out that only Singapore and Hong Kong didn't show finest model in model (8) whatever based on the testing result of BPN or RBFNN. In addition, Table 15 denotes the empirical results for China. The best model for BPN is Model (6), although in the case of China didn't support full variables in BPN but it has better performance for model (8) in RBFNN.

Table 6 Summary of BPN and RBFNN results for Japan

Japan (BPN)		Model(1)	Model(2)	Model(3)	Model(4)	Model(5)	Model(6)	Model(7)	**Model(8)
Hidden Nodes: 15	Samples	55	55	55	55	55	55	55	**55**
Hidden Layer: 1	MSE	0.00068	0.00027	0.00170	0.00046	0.00015	0.00009	0.00043	**0.00007**
Maximum Epochs: 100,000	NMSE	0.01472	0.00573	0.03688	0.00991	0.00320	0.00200	0.00926	**0.00170**
Learning rate: 0.5	R^2	0.99312	0.99747	0.98301	0.99571	0.99918	0.99970	0.99745	**0.99953**
Japan (RBFNN)		Model(1)	Model(2)	Model(3)	Model(4)	**Model(5)	Model(6)	Model(7)	Model(8)
Hidden Nodes: 15	Samples	55	55	55	55	**55**	55	55	55
Hidden Layer: 1	MSE	0.00749	0.00560	0.00527	0.00718	**0.00464**	0.00860	0.00588	0.00634
Maximum Epochs: 20,000	NMSE	0.16216	0.12229	0.11412	0.15547	**0.10053**	0.18614	0.12733	0.13726
Learning rate: 0.5	R^2	0.91949	0.93720	0.94234	0.92089	**0.94873**	0.90602	0.94116	0.92886

Note: 1. **indicates better performance consequence based on the testing criteria of MSE and NMSE.

2. In a wake of testing the epochs effect for RBFNN model, the result of 10,000 iterative epochs shows pretty close outcome with 100,000 iterative test. We consider utilizing 10,000 iterative epochs for RBFNN model.

Table 7 Summary of BPN and RBFNN results for Indonesia

Indonesia (BPN)		Model(1)	Model(2)	Model(3)	Model(4)	Model(5)	Model(6)	Model(7)	**Model(8)
Hidden Nodes: 15	Samples	55	55	55	55	55	55	55	**55**
Hidden Layer: 1	MSE	0.00307	0.00010	0.00047	0.00320	0.00021	0.00010	0.00010	**0.00006**
Maximum Epochs: 100,000	NMSE	0.04511	0.00151	0.00692	0.00469	0.00311	0.00153	0.00149	**0.00096**
Learning rate: 0.5	R^2	0.97728	0.99934	0.99700	0.99765	0.99877	0.99923	0.99943	**0.99952**
Indonesia (RBFNN)		Model(1)	Model(2)	Model(3)	Model(4)	**Model(5)	Model(6)	Model(7)	Model(8)
Hidden Nodes: 15	Samples	55	55	55	55	**55**	55	55	55
Hidden Layer: 1	MSE	0.00346	0.00296	0.00300	0.00437	**0.00262**	0.00446	0.00337	0.00343
Maximum Epochs: 20,000	NMSE	0.05091	0.04352	0.04415	0.06428	**0.03855**	0.06549	0.04951	0.05044
Learning rate: 0.5	R^2	0.97465	0.97857	0.97814	0.96770	**0.98121**	0.96676	0.97594	0.97590

Note: 1. **indicates better performance consequence based on the testing criteria of MSE and NMSE.

2. In a wake of testing the epochs effect for RBFNN model, the result of 10,000 iterative epochs shows pretty close outcome with 100,000 iterative test. We consider utilizing 10,000 iterative epochs for RBFNN model.

Table 8 Summary of BPN and RBFNN results for Taiwan

Taiwan (BPN)		Model(1)	Model(2)	Model(3)	Model(4)	Model(5)	Model(6)	Model(7)	**Model(8)
Hidden Nodes: 3	Samples	55	55	55	55	55	55	55	**55**
Hidden Layer: 1	MSE	0.01114	0.02145	0.00330	0.01418	0.00300	0.01355	0.00365	**0.00196**
Maximum Epochs: 100,000	NMSE	0.11274	0.21708	0.03347	0.14352	0.03045	0.13710	0.03693	**0.01983**
Learning rate: 0.5	R^2	0.94375	0.89403	0.98367	0.92810	0.98479	0.93291	0.98179	**0.99120**
Taiwan (RBFNN)		Model(1)	Model(2)	Model(3)	Model(4)	**Model(5)	Model(6)	Model(7)	Model(8)
Hidden Nodes: 3	Samples	55	55	55	55	**55**	55	55	55
Hidden Layer: 1	MSE	0.02408	0.03193	0.00365	0.01812	**0.00355**	0.01502	0.00396	0.00538
Maximum Epochs: 20,000	NMSE	0.06090	0.32309	0.03697	0.18338	**0.03596**	0.15201	0.04016	0.01360
Learning rate: 0.5	R^2	0.97108	0.83798	0.98138	0.90791	**0.98204**	0.92165	0.98504	0.99322

Note: 1. **indicates better performance consequence based on the testing criteria of MSE and NMSE.

2. In a wake of testing the epochs effect for RBFNN model, the result of 10,000 iterative epochs shows pretty close outcome with 100,000 iterative test. We consider utilizing 10,000 iterative epochs for RBFNN model.

Table 9 Summary of BPN and RBFNN results for Korea

Korea (BPN)		Model(1)	Model(2)	Model(3)	Model(4)	**Model(5)	Model(6)	Model(7)	Model(8)
Hidden Nodes: 7	Samples	55	55	55	55	**55**	55	55	55
Hidden Layer: 1	MSE	0.00095	0.00099	0.00092	0.00058	**0.00010**	0.00059	0.00142	0.00014
Maximum Epochs: 100,000	NMSE	0.01152	0.01193	0.01118	0.00070	**0.00127**	0.00715	0.01712	0.00173
Learning rate: 0.5	R^2	0.99440	0.99432	0.99471	0.99694	**0.99969**	0.99669	0.99164	0.99928
Korea (RBFNN)		Model(1)	Model(2)	Model(3)	Model(4)	Model(5)	Model(6)	Model(7)	**Model(8)
Hidden Nodes: 7	Samples	55	55	55	55	55	55	55	**55**
Hidden Layer: 1	MSE	0.00509	0.00311	0.00439	0.00503	0.00348	0.00329	0.00307	**0.00291**
Maximum Epochs: 20,000	NMSE	0.05328	0.03252	0.04588	0.05266	0.03639	0.03444	0.03210	**0.03044**
Learning rate: 0.5	R^2	0.97319	0.98362	0.97840	0.97649	0.98190	0.98399	0.98421	**0.98481**

Note: 1. **indicates better performance consequence based on the testing criteria of MSE and NMSE.

2. In a wake of testing the epochs effect for RBFNN model, the result of 10,000 iterative epochs shows pretty close outcome with 100,000 iterative test. We consider utilizing 10,000 iterative epochs for RBFNN model.

52

Table 10 Summary of BPN and RBFNN results for Malaysia

Malaysia (BPN)		Model(1)	Model(2)	Model(3)	Model(4)	Model(5)	Model(6)	Model(7)	**Model(8)
Hidden Nodes: 7	Samples	55	55	55	55	55	55	55	55
Hidden Layer: 1	MSE	0.00294	0.00199	0.00056	0.00055	0.00043	0.00123	0.00035	0.00028
Maximum Epochs: 100,000	NMSE	0.03081	0.02086	0.00590	0.00580	0.00449	0.01294	0.00371	0.00298
Learning rate: 0.5	R^2	0.98591	0.98965	0.99730	0.99710	0.99779	0.99352	0.99832	0.99864
Malaysia (RBFNN)		Model(1)	Model(2)	Model(3)	Model(4)	Model(5)	Model(6)	Model(7)	**Model(8)
Hidden Nodes: 7	Samples	55	55	55	55	55	55	55	55
Hidden Layer: 1	MSE	0.01426	0.00646	0.01376	0.01059	0.00791	0.00858	0.00776	0.00385
Maximum Epochs: 20,000	NMSE	0.40624	0.18402	0.39194	0.30183	0.22527	0.24447	0.22127	0.10964
Learning rate: 0.5	R^2	0.77871	0.90317	0.78275	0.83653	0.88076	0.86921	0.88254	0.94436

Note: 1. **indicates better performance consequence based on the testing criteria of MSE and NMSE.

2. In a wake of testing the epochs effect for RBFNN model, the result of 10,000 iterative epochs shows pretty close outcome with 100,000 iterative test. We consider utilizing 10,000 iterative epochs for RBFNN model.

Table 11 Summary of BPN and RBFNN results for Philippines

Philippines (BPN)		Model(1)	Model(2)	Model(3)	Model(4)	Model(5)	Model(6)	Model(7)	**Model(8)
Hidden Nodes: 13	Samples	55	55	55	55	55	55	55	**55**
Hidden Layer: 1	MSE	0.00384	0.00154	0.00033	0.00026	0.00039	0.00611	0.00015	**0.00001**
Maximum Epochs: 100,000	NMSE	0.00456	0.01829	0.00394	0.00318	0.00472	0.07258	0.00185	**0.00022**
Learning rate: 0.5	R^2	0.97717	0.99081	0.99811	0.99889	0.99831	0.96380	0.99939	**0.99990**
Philippines (RBFNN)		Model(1)	Model(2)	Model(3)	Model(4)	Model(5)	**Model(6)	Model(7)	Model(8)
Hidden Nodes: 13	Samples	55	55	55	55	55	**55**	55	55
Hidden Layer: 1	MSE	0.00662	0.00494	0.00689	0.00506	0.00262	**0.00144**	0.00426	0.00203
Maximum Epochs: 20,000	NMSE	0.07861	0.05872	0.08187	0.06019	0.03115	**0.01720**	0.05063	0.02410
Learning rate: 0.5	R^2	0.96063	0.97186	0.95851	0.97027	0.98440	**0.99182**	0.97468	0.98837

Note: 1. **indicates better performance consequence based on the testing criteria of MSE and NMSE.

2. In a wake of testing the epochs effect for RBFNN model, the result of 10,000 iterative epochs shows pretty close outcome with 100,000 iterative test. We consider utilizing 10,000 iterative epochs for RBFNN model.

Table 12 Summary of BPN and RBFNN results for Thailand

Thailand (BPN)		Model(1)	Model(2)	Model(3)	Model(4)	Model(5)	Model(6)	Model(7)	**Model(8)
Hidden Nodes: 9	Samples	55	55	55	55	55	55	55	**55**
Hidden Layer: 1	MSE	0.00202	0.00148	0.00083	0.00037	0.00031	0.00040	0.00061	**0.00008**
Maximum Epochs: 100,000	NMSE	0.01871	0.01377	0.00771	0.00346	0.00295	0.00375	0.00570	**0.00081**
Learning rate: 0.1	R^2	0.99073	0.99313	0.99614	0.99837	0.99888	0.99841	0.99733	**0.99961**
Thailand (RBFNN)		Model(1)	Model(2)	Model(3)	Model(4)	Model(5)	**Model(6)	Model(7)	Model(8)
Hidden Nodes: 9	Samples	55	55	55	55	55	**55**	55	55
Hidden Layer: 1	MSE	0.00202	0.00195	0.00277	0.00234	0.002985	**0.00085**	0.00159	0.00222
Maximum Epochs: 20,000	NMSE	0.01871	0.01808	0.02570	0.02169	0.027653	**0.00788**	0.01479	0.02062
Learning rate: 0.1	R^2	0.99060	0.99110	0.98707	0.98928	0.986331	**0.99632**	0.99259	0.99014

Note: 1. **indicates better performance consequence based on the testing criteria of MSE and NMSE.

2. In a wake of testing the epochs effect for RBFNN model, the result of 10,000 iterative epochs shows pretty close outcome with 100,000 iterative test. We consider utilizing 10,000 iterative epochs for RBFNN model.

Table 13 Summary of BPN and RBFNN results for Singapore

Singapore (BPN)		Model(1)	Model(2)	Model(3)	Model(4)	**Model(5)	Model(6)	Model(7)	Model(8)
Hidden Nodes: 15	Samples	55	55	55	55	55	55	55	55
Hidden Layer: 1	MSE	0.02402	0.02443	0.01486	0.01017	0.00176	0.00458	0.00277	0.00186
Maximum Epochs: 100,000	NMSE	0.74017	0.75279	0.45805	0.31361	0.05433	0.14112	0.08540	0.05732
Learning rate: 0.1	R^2	0.54489	0.54383	0.75298	0.82907	0.97476	0.92934	0.96682	0.97218
Singapore (RBFNN)		Model(1)	Model(2)	Model(3)	Model(4)	Model(5)	Model(6)	**Model(7)	Model(8)
Hidden Nodes: 15	Samples	55	55	55	55	55	55	55	55
Hidden Layer: 1	MSE	0.02966	0.02925	0.02384	0.02753	0.02470	0.03428	0.02010	0.02116
Maximum Epochs: 20,000	NMSE	0.91389	0.90113	0.73453	0.84837	0.76116	1.05616	0.61926	0.65192
Learning rate: 0.1	R^2	0.41369	0.44074	0.56643	0.45435	0.50893	0.23476	0.63887	0.60205

Note: 1. **indicates better performance consequence based on the testing criteria of MSE and NMSE.

2. In a wake of testing the epochs effect for RBFNN model, the result of 10,000 iterative epochs shows pretty close outcome with 100,000 iterative test. We consider utilizing 10,000 iterative epochs for RBFNN model.

Table 14 Summary of BPN and RBFNN results for Hong Kong

Hong Kong (BPN)		Model(1)	Model(2)	Model(3)	Model(4)	Model(5)	Model(6)	**Model(7)	Model(8)
Hidden Nodes: 7	Samples	55	55	55	55	55	55	**55**	55
Hidden Layer: 1	MSE	0.00513	0.00601	0.00202	0.00547	0.00133	0.00621	**0.00083**	0.00398
Maximum Epochs: 100,000	NMSE	0.13876	0.16233	0.05463	0.14780	0.03591	0.16778	**0.02251**	0.10768
Learning rate: 0.05	R^2	0.93090	0.91924	0.97287	0.92612	0.98406	0.91706	**0.99226**	0.94619
Hong Kong (RBFNN)		**Model(1)**	**Model(2)**	**Model(3)**	**Model(4)**	***Model(5)**	**Model(6)**	**Model(7)**	**Model(8)**
Hidden Nodes: 7	Samples	55	55	55	55	**55**	55	55	55
Hidden Layer: 1	MSE	0.02315	0.01978	0.01870	0.01876	**0.00678**	0.02035	0.00744	0.01651
Maximum Epochs: 20,000	NMSE	0.62531	0.53427	0.50512	0.50666	**0.18311**	0.54958	0.20115	0.44592
Learning rate: 0.05	R^2	0.61987	0.68554	0.71002	0.72710	**0.91353**	0.68260	0.90217	0.76221

Note: 1. **indicates better performance consequence based on the testing criteria of MSE and NMSE.
2. In a wake of testing the epochs effect for RBFNN model, the result of 10,000 iterative epochs shows pretty close outcome with 100,000 iterative test. We consider utilizing 10,000 iterative epochs for RBFNN model.

Table 15 Summary of BPN and RBFNN results for China

China (BPN)		Model(1)	Model(2)	Model(3)	Model(4)	Model(5)	**Model(6)	Model(7)	Model(8)
Hidden Nodes: 5	Samples	55	55	55	55	55	55	55	55
Hidden Layer: 1	MSE	0.01399	0.00902	0.00471	0.00466	0.00314	**0.00160**	0.00162	0.00210
Maximum Epochs: 100,000	NMSE	0.39864	0.25712	0.13418	0.13282	0.08952	**0.04579**	0.04620	0.05989
Learning rate: 0.05	R^2	0.78254	0.86807	0.93820	0.93470	0.95853	**0.97691**	0.97941	0.97152
China (RBFNN)		Model(1)	Model(2)	Model(3)	Model(4)	Model(5)	Model(6)	Model(7)	**Model(8)
Hidden Nodes: 5	Samples	55	55	55	55	55	55	55	**55**
Hidden Layer: 1	MSE	0.01673	0.00848	0.00933	0.01828	0.00755	0.01151	0.01011	**0.00754**
Maximum Epochs: 20,000	NMSE	0.47671	0.24170	0.26589	0.52079	0.21520	0.32796	0.28814	**0.21502**
Learning rate: 0.05	R^2	0.73168	0.87674	0.86331	0.69921	0.88710	0.82919	0.84616	**0.88940**

Note: 1. **indicates better performance consequence based on the testing criteria of MSE and NMSE.
2. In a wake of testing the epochs effect for RBFNN model, the result cf 10,000 iterative epochs shows pretty close outcome with 100,000 iterative test. We consider utilizing 10,000 iterative epochs for RBFNN model.

58

To further confirm the effectiveness for optimal components of ACU, we compare the empirical results of BPN with RBFNN model. Table 16 indicates the synopsis information for BPN and RBFNN estimations. Overall, model (8) has the most outstanding performance in terms of BPN testing. There are six countries (such as Japan, Indonesia, Malaysia, Philippines, Thailand and Taiwan) equipped with high explanatory power and the lowest error value in model (8). Relatively, Model (5) represents better performance in RBFNN model in terms of Japan, Hong Kong, Indonesia and Taiwan. Obviously, we found that the performance of BPN is superior to RBFNN, because the testing results in MSE and NMSE of BPN are significant lower than the RBFNN model. In addition, the drawback of RBFNN demonstrated some limitation for its input value. When the input data shows great distance away from the center of cluster data, it generates over volatility for gaussian function so as to receive the inferior results in RBFNN model. In the case of the optimal components analysis, our macro-controls data has far away from the center points. Under this situation, the estimating performance of RBFNN is poorer than BPN model (Donald and Krzysztof, 1996).

Table 16 Synopsis of BPN and RBFN results in connection with optimal components analysis of central value of ACU

Country	Back-Propagation neural network (BPN)	Radial Basis Function Neural Network (RBFNN)
Japan	Model 8 MSE (0.00007) NMSE (0.00170)	Model 5 MSE (0.00464) NMSE (0.10053)
Hong Kong	Model 7 MSE (0.00083) NMSE (0.02251)	Model 5 MSE (0.00678) NMSE (0.18311)
Indonesia	Model 8 MSE (0.00006) NMSE (0.00096)	Model 5 MSE (0.00262) NMSE (0.03855)
Korea	Model 5 MSE (0.00010) NMSE (0.00127)	Model 8 MSE (0.00291) NMSE (0.03044)
Malaysia	Model 8 MSE (0.0002854) NMSE (0.0029829)	Model 8 MSE (0.0038500) NMSE (0.1096499)
Philippines	Model 8 MSE (0.00001) NMSE (0.00022)	Model 6 MSE (0.00144) NMSE (0.01720)
Thailand	Model 8 MSE (0.00008) NMSE (0.00081)	Model 6 MSE (0.000850) NMSE (0.00788)
Singapore	Model 5 MSE (0.0017636) NMSE (0.054332)	Model 7 MSE (0.0201010) NMSE (0.6192673)
China	Model 6 MSE (0.00160) NMSE (0.04579)	Model 8 MSE (0.00754) NMSE (0.21502)
Taiwan	Model 8 MSE (0.00196) NMSE (0.01983)	Model 5 MSE (0.00355) NMSE (0.03962)

According to the empirical result of BPN model in Tables 16, Japan, Indonesia, Malaysia, Philippines, Thailand and Taiwan could take the ratio of foreign direct investment to GDP, the ratio of external debt to GDP and the ratio of bank's claim on private sector to GDP into account to establish the central weights of ACU. Korea and Singapore are better to consider adding the ratio of foreign direct investment to GDP and the ratio of external debt to GDP in terms of the central weights. The manipulation components for China need to further accede the ratio of FDI to GDP and the ratio of bank's claim on private sector to GDP. The optimal components for Hong Kong are jointing the ratio of external debt to GDP and the ratio of bank's claim on private sector to GDP to basis pattern. It is worth to notice that China announced the reference basket components which contained trade value, external debt and foreign direct investment etc. However, we compare the report for China's reference basket components with our empirical results of BPN[22]. The prime basket components constitution is model (6) excluded the importance of external debt regarding to the central weight of ACU for China. In other words, to eliminate external debt from basket components of ACU for China could further improve the components of ACU in terms of reflecting central weight for China.

4.3. The empirical results for contagion cause

In this section, we analyze the main contagion causes in Asia Finances Crisis. Based on previous discussion, there is very likelihood that contagion has been broken out because of the change in similar macroeconomic fundament, trade linkage and financial linkage. Our study flow path in this part could briefly introduce in Figure 17. In order to comprehensively analyze the impact on contagion causes for Asian countries, we design the testing model into seven cause combinations, including TRA, FIN, M.S., TRA & FIN, TRA & M.S., FIN & M.S. and full-input model which contains three contagion cause variables. The analysis tool for contagion causes discussion is ANFIS model. The Member Functions (MFs) per input value determines the number of membership functions which assigned to each network input. In this study, after we compare the testing performance and epoch time, we establish 2 for MFs is most suitable for our sample size. Table 16 illustrates the testing results for contagion analysis. Our estimating criterion is MSE and NMSE values.

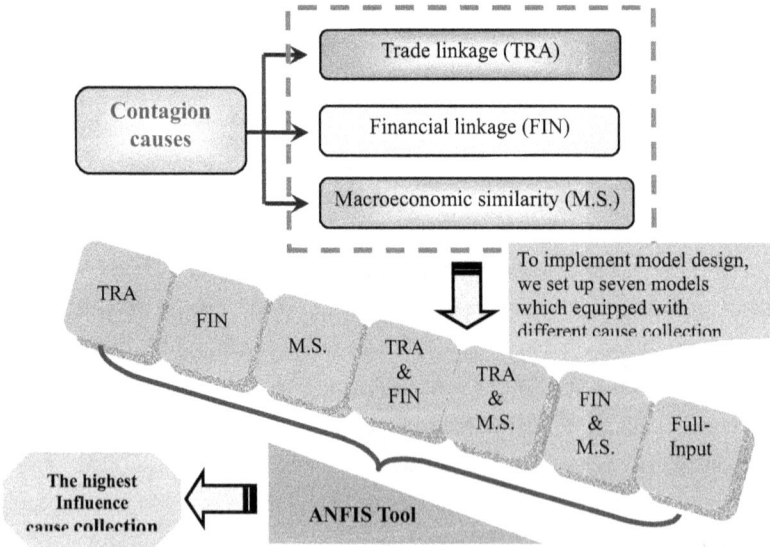

Figure 17. The research flow path for contagion causes analysis

---

[22] Source: Economic Daily (2005/8/11), "Which basket currencies that Renminbi take it into account".

Table 17 Testing outcome for contagion cause analysis in ANFIS model

Parameters Setting	Trade Linkage	Financial Linkage	Macroeconomic Similarity	Trade and Financial	Trade and Macroeconomic Similarity	Financial and Macroeconomic Similarity	Full-Input model
Input values	1	1	5	2	6	6	7
Membership Function	Bell Function	Bell Function	Bell Function	Bell Function	Bell Function	Bell Function	Bell Function
MFs per Input	2	2	2	2	2	2	2
Transfer Function	Sigmoid Function	Sigmoid Function	Sigmoid Function	Sigmoid Function	Sigmoid Function	Sigmoid Function	Sigmoid Function
Fuzzy Rule	TSK	TSK	TSK	TSK	TSK	TSK	TSK
Learning Rate	0.1	0.1	0.1	0.1	0.1	0.1	0.1
Maximum Epochs	10,000	10,000	10,000	10,000	10,000	10,000	10,000
MSE	0.1794	0.2018	0.0066	0.1860	0.0597	**0.0040	0.0778
NMSE	1.2812	1.3284	0.0337	1.2938	0.3228	**0.0217	0.4322
R^2	0.0346	0.6391	0.9422	0.4128	0.7506	**0.9842	0.7591

Note: 1. ** represents better performance consequence based on the testing criteria of MSE and NMSE.

2. Trade Linkage has only one input value and Financial Linkage has one input value also. There are five Macroeconomic variables to be represent Macroeconomic Similarity.

3. TSK fuzzy model was known as Sugeno fuzzy model.

According to the estimations of ANFIS, we find a very different empirical result when weight against previous researches. Foe example, Van Rijckeghem and Weder (2001) found that the financial linkage plays the most critical factor in terms of contagion occurrence via probit regression. However, our findings reveal that the contagion effect could fully express via financial linkage combined with the macroeconomic similarity inputs. When financial system destabilization will let creditor nations such as Japan unable to receive their loans from debtor nations such as Thailand. Consequently, this may cause spillover effect to nearly Asian countries. On the other hand, the profile of macroeconomic structure has explanation power in this study. It demonstrates that five macroeconomic variables (such as the ratio of M2 to international reserves, the current account balance as a percent of GDP, the ratio of government budget deficit (surplus) to GDP, the ratio of short-term debt to reserve and discount rate for each country) could illustrate contagion process effectively. Moreover, the macroeconomic similarity has higher influence than Trade linkage. This result shows opposed perspective of relatively sequence with Glick and Rose (1999), Van Rijkeghem and Weder (2001) and Leonardo and Rodrigo (2001).

Chapter 5. Conclusion and Suggestion

5.1. Conclusion

In regard to the performance for exchange rate forecasting tool, our sample forecasting period of ACU against U.S. Dollars was covered from March 2, 1992 to June 30, 2005. We have set up 20% testing, 25% testing, 30% testing, 40% testing, 45% testing and 50% testing data. The BPN model shows the best performance in 20%, 25%, 30% and 40% calculations and the TDRNN model was equipped with outstanding performance in 45% and 50% calculations. Moreover, the ANN tools have superior performance than the GARCH (1, 1) model.

This paper has provided empirical analysis for modified components of ACU via artificial neural network. In light of the constitution components of Asian currency unit was been comprehensive discussed in recent year, the results of this study likely verify the basket components for participants of ACU. We have choose ten currencies of nine Asian countries to be our research sample such as Japan, Indonesia, Hong Kong, Malaysia, Philippines, South Korea, Singapore, Thailand, China and Taiwan. In this part, we employ quarterly macroeconomic information which was covered from first quarter, 1992 to second quarter, 2005. Our empirical evidence suggests that the three new adding macro-variables such as foreign direct investment, external debt and bank's claim on private sector could effectively enhance the ANN models' explanation ability for ACU with the original macroeconomic-controls such as export volume, net reverse and GDP per capita. The testing models which contain new adding macro-variables have the lower value of MSE and NMSE than the basis model.

According to the empirical results, the BPN has better performance and model explanation ability than the RBFNN model. More importantly, with the prominent training and learning capability the BPN model was equipped with higher fault tolerant capability than the RBFNN model.

In regard to the analysis of contagion causes, we employ three years data which one year before and after the finances flu in 1997. According to the empirical finding for this part, the financial linkage and macroeconomic similarity are cardinal reasons to cause the contagion effect when flared up Asia Flu. This result isn't coincidence with Eichengreen and Wypolsz (1996), Glick and Rose (1999) and Van Rijckeghem and Weder (2001), Leonardo and Rodrigo (2001). However, we proof the important for financial lending relation and profile of macroeconomic similarity between Asian countries via ANFIS model to be the empirical tool.

To summary the main contribution of this research could categorized into three points, firstly, we proof that ANNs model has better outperformance in ACU forecasting than GARCH (1, 1). Moreover, we demonstrated that BPN model shows greater forecasting performance in most of division cases. Secondly, three new adding macroeconomic variables have effectively express

64

ability for modifying the basket components of ACU. Lastly, by discussing the contagion causes for Asia flu, we utilize ANFIS model to analyze this topic and find different empirical results when weight against Eichengreen and Wypolsz (1996), Glick and Rose (1999) and Van Rijckeghem and Weder (2001), Leonardo and Rodrigo (2001) who by using probit regression. The financial linkage and macroeconomic similarity could be explained the contagion source for Asia flu significantly.

5.2. Research Restriction

1. Two of main output values in this study are concentrated on the central weights of Asian currency unit and exchange rate of Asian currency unit when weight against U.S. dollars. We conduct simulation for ACU and started based on started year of Maastricht Treaty which created EU in 1992. In light of modified components analysis for ACU and forecasting performance of AUC, it may imply the problem of factualness deficiency due to our simulation value of ACU was followed by the mode of Euro. Therefore, the completeness of constitution process of ACU needs to be further considered.

2. With regard to selecting for sample countries, we exclude some members of ASEAN such as Myanmar and Brunei mainly because it's tough to collect their macroeconomic data. Eventually, we choose ten currencies among nine Asian countries to our research samples.

3. In regard to macroeconomic variables selecting for modified components of ACU, the authority of Mainland China didn't fully pronounce reference components for Renminbi basket. This condition generates restriction for variables employing. In this section, we only utilize six macroeconomic variables to analyze the modified components of ACU. It may not completely express the empirical results for modified components.

5.3. Research Suggestion

1. In order to fully express the optimal basket components of ACU, it should consider enrich the sample country in Asia or near Asia area. For example, except for some member countries of ASEAN such as Myanmar, Laos, Vietnam and Brunei, to follow the member developed condition of ASEAN one may take India, New Zealand and even Russia into account.

2. In this study we utilize error back-propagation algorithm to find out the connection weights in hidden layer for BPN model. In terms of finest weight searching, Genetic Algorithm could combine with ANN model to reach best empirical results.

3. With regard to variables of optimal components analysis of ACU, it could further consider some other macroeconomic-controls or dummy variables. For instance, country's credit ratings could esteem as a dummy variable to analyze the possibility of increasing modified performance to basket components of ACU.

The thirteen years tendency of ACU

ACU/USD

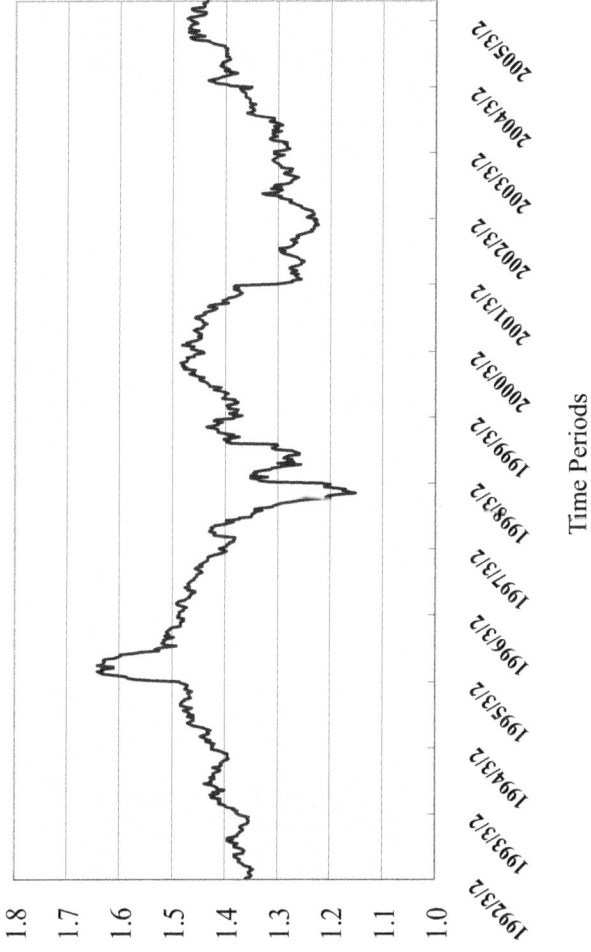

Time Periods

Reference

Andreou, A. S., G. F., Efstratios and L. D., Spirdon, 2002. Exchange-Rates Forecasting: A Hybrid Algorithm Based on Genetically Optimized Adaptive Neural Network, Computational Economics, 20, 191-210.

Bayoumi, Tamim and Mauro, Paolo, 2001. The Suitability of ASEAN for a Regional Currency Arrangement, The World Economy, 24, 933.

Broomhead, D. S. and D., Lowe, 1998. Multivarible Function Interpolation and Adaptive Network, Complex Syst, 2, 321-335.

Bollerslev, T., 1986. Generalized Autoregressive Conditional Heteroscedasticity, Journal of Econometrics, 31, 307-327.

Bratsiotis, George J. and Robinson, Wayne, 2004. Economic Fundamentals and Self-fulfilling Crises: Further Evidence from Mexico, Journal of International Money and Finance, 23, 595-613.

Caporale, Tony and Doroodian, Khosrow, 1994. Exchange Rate Variability and the Flow of International Trade, Economics Letters, 46, 49-54.

Chang, Fi-John and Huang, Hau Lung, 2003. Theory and Practice of Artificial Neural Network, Dong Hwa Publication.

Chang, Chun-Hung, 2004. Pricing Euro Currency Options — Comparison of Back Propagation Neural Network Model and Recurrenct Neural Network Model. Graduate School of Business Administration, Chung Yuan Christian University, Taiwan. (In Chinese)

Chen, Chien-Shun, 1999. The Research on the Impact of Asian Economic Storm on the Volatility in Major Float Currencies (Focus on Yen and Mark). Graduate Institute of Business Administration, National ChungHsing University, Taiwan. (In Chinese)

Chen, Jo-Hui and Chen, Chih-Sean, 2006. The Formation of Asian Optimum Currency Area and the Empirical Study of Exchange Rate Target Zone, Journal of Innovation and Management, 3 (1), 71-98. (In Chinese)

Chen, Jo-Hui and Hsieh, Hsin Han, 2004. The Study of Relationship between Asian Currency Unification and Trade, Asia Pacific Review of Social Science and Technology, 3 (2), 87-117. (In Chinese)

Chen, Shu-Ju, 2001. The Evaluation Analysis of Asian Currency Unit (ACU) Mechanism-The Study of Integration for Asian Countries Economic Variables. Graduate School of Business Administration, Chung Yuan Christian University, Taiwan. (In Chinese)

Cybenko, G., 1989. Approximation by Superposition of a Sigmoidal Function, Math, Control Systems Signal, 2, 303-314.

Donald, K., Wedding II. and Krzysztof J., Cios, 1996. Time Series Forecasting by Combining RBF Network, Certainty Factors, and the Box-Jenkins Model, Neruocomputing, 10, 149-168.

Dutta, M., 2002. Asian Economic Community Intra-Community, Micro and Macro-Economic Parameters, Journal of Asia Economics, 13(4), 447-491.

Eichengreen, B., Rose, A. K. and Wypolsz, C., 1996. Contagious Currency Crisis: First Tests, Scandinavian Journal of Economics, 98, 463-484.

Engle, R.F., 1982. Autoregressive Conditional Heteroscedaticity with Estimates of the Variance of United Kingdom Inflation, Econometrica, 50, 987-1008.

Eric, Rahimian, Seema, Singh, Thongchai, Thammachote, and Rajiv, Virmani, 1996. Bankruptcy Prediction by Neural Network, Neural Networks in Finance and Investing Using Artificial Intelligence to Improve Real-World Performance. R. R. Trippi and E. Turban, Chicago: Irwin, USA.

Flood, Robert P. and Marion, Nancy, 1996. Speculative Attacks: Fundamentals and Self-fulfilling Prophecies, NBER Working Paper., No. 5789.

Frankel, J.A. and Rose, A. K., 1996. Currency Crashes in Emerging Markets: An Empirical Treatment, Journal of International Economics, 41, 351-366.

Frattale, Mascioli F. M. and Martinelli, G., 1998. A Constructive Approach to Neuro-Fuzzy Networks, Signal Processing, 64, 347-358.

Glick, R. and Rose, A.K., 1999. Contagion and Trade Why are Currency Crises Regional? Journal of International Money and Finance, 18, 603-617.

Greg, Tkacz, 2001. Neural Network Forecasting of Canadian GDP Growth, International Journal of Forecasting, 17, 57-69.

Haish, Wen-Yi, 2004. The Study of Relationship between Central Rate of Asian Currency Unit and the Currency Crises Warning Model. Graduate School of Business Administration, Chung Yuan Christian University, Taiwan. (In Chinese)

Harald, Sander and Stefanie, Kleimeier, 2003. Contagion and Causality: An Empirical Investigation of Four Asian Crisis Episodes, Journal of International Financial Markets Institutions & Money, 13, 171-186.

Hecht-Nielsen, R., 1990. Applications of Counter Propagation Networks, Neural Networks, 1, 131-139.

Hu, Michael Y. and Christos, Tsoukalas, 1999. Combining Conditional Volatility Forecasts Using Neural Networks: An Application to the EMS Exchange Rates, Journal of International Financial Markets, Institutions and Money, 9, 407-422.

Hwang, Jing-Terg, 1998. The Impact of East Asia Financial Crisis in Primary Daily Foreign Exchange Rates on Volatility, Graduate Institute of Business Administration, National Chung Hsing University, Taiwan. (In Chinese)

Hyuk, Choe, Bong-Chan, Kho, and Rene, M., Stulz, 1999. Do Foreign Investors Destabilize Stock Markets? The Korean Experience in 1997, Journal of Financial Economics, 54, 227-264.

Jang, Jyh-Shing, 1993. ANFIS: Adaptive-Network-Based Fuzzy Inference System, MAN, and Cybernetics, 23, 665-684.

Jang, Jyh-Shing and Sun, Chuen-Tsai, 1995. Neuro-Fuzzy Modeling and Control, The Proceedings of the IEEE, 83, 378-406.

Jang, Jyh-Shing, Sun, Chuen-Tsai and Mizutani, E., 1997. Neuro-Fuzzy and Soft Computing: A Computational Approach to Learning and Machine Intelligence, Matlab Curriculum Series. Prentice-Hall International Inc.: Upper Saddle River, N. J.

Jeanne, Olivier, 1997. Are Currency Self-fulfilling? A Test, Journal of Internaional Economics, 43, 263-286.

Jorge, V. Perez-Rodriguez, Salvador, Torra and Julian, Andrada-Felix, 2005. STAR and ANN Models: Forcasting Performance on the Spanish "Ibex-35" Stock Index, Journal of Empirical Finance, 12, 490-509.

Joseph, Plasmans, Willian, Verkooijen and Hennie, Daniels, 1998. Estimating Structural Exchange Rate Models by Artificial Neural Networks, Applied Financial Economics, 8, 541-551.

Kaminsky, Graciela, Lizondo, Saul and Reinhart, Carmen M., 1997. Leading Indicators of Currency Crises, NBER Working Paper, 97/79.

Kecman, V., 2001. Learning and Soft Computing: Support Vector Machines, Neural Networks, and Fuzzy Logic Models, Cambridge, MA: MIT Press.

Kim, Sung-Suk, 1998. Time-Delay Recurrent Neural Network for Temporal Correlations and Prediction, Neurocomputing, 20, 253-263.

Knenneth, D. West and Dongchul, Cho, 1995. The Predictive Ability of Several Models of Exchange Rate Volatility, Journal of Econometrics, 69, 367-391.

Kenneth, S. Chan, Chi-Chur, Chao, and Win, Lin Chou, 2002. Trade Similarities and Contagion among the Asian Crisis Economies, Journal of Asian Economics, 13, 271-283.

Krugman, Paul R., 1979. A model of Balance-of-Payments Crises, Journal of Money, Credit, and Banking, 11, 311-325.

Krugman, Paul R., 1991. Target Zones and Exchange Rate Dynamic, The Quarterly Journal of Economics, 3, 669-682.

Kuan, C. M. and White, H., 1994. Artificial Neural Networks: An Econometric Perspective, Econometric Reviews, 13, 1-91.

Leonardo, F. Hernandez and Rodrigo, O. Valdes, 2001. What Drive Contagion Trade, Neighborhood, or Financial Links? International Review of Financial Analysis, 10, 203-218.

Leung, Mark T., An-Sing, Chen, and Hazem, Daouk, 2000. Forecasting Exchange Rates Using General Regression Neural Networks, Computers & Operations Research, 27, 1093-1110.

Letiche, J. M., 2000. Lessons from the Euro Zone for the East Asian Economics, Journal of Asian Economics, 11, 276-300.

Marais, E. and Bates, S., 2005. An Empirical Study to Identify Shift Contagion during the Asian Crisis, Journal of International Financial Markets, Institutions & Money, Working Paper.

Massimliano, Marcellino, 2004. Forecasting EMU Macroeconomic Variables, International Journal of Forecasting, 20, 359-372.

Mohan, Kumar, Uma, Moorthy and William, Perraudin, 2003. Predicting Emerging Market Currency Crashes, Journal of Empirical Finance, 10, 427-454.

Monica, Lam, 2004. Neural Network Techniques for Financial Performance Prediction: Integration Fundamental and Technical Analysis, Decision Support Systems, 37, 567-581.

Nayak, P. C., K. P., Sudheer, D. M., Rangan, and K. S., Ramasastri, 2004. A Neuro-Fuzzy Computing Technique for Modeling Hydrological Time Series, Journal of Hydrology, 291, 52-66.

Nieh, Chien-Chung, Fung, Jeng-An and Kuo, Chi-Liang, 2001. Forecasting the Exchange of N.T. Dollars for U.S. Dollars in Financial Crisis-An Application of Back-Propagation Neural Network, Journal of Taiwanese Finance, 2 (3), 119-146. (In Chinese)

Odom, M. D. and R., Sharda, 1990. A Neural Network for Bankruptcy Prediction, International Joint Conference on Neural Networks, 2, 163-168.

Powell, M. J. D., 1987. Radial Basis Functions For Multivariable Interpolation: A Review. IMA Conference on Algorithms for Approximation of Functions and Data. RMCS, Shrivenham, England. 143-167.

Qi, Min and Zhang, G. P., 2001. An Investigation of Model Selection Criteria for Neural Network Time Series Forecasting, European Journal of Operational Research, 132, 666-680.

Raj, Aggarwal and Mbodja, Mougoue, 1996. Cointegration among Asian Currencies: Evidence of the Increasing Influence of the Japanese Yen, Japan and World Economy, 291~308.

Rauscher, F. A., 1997. Exchange Rate Forecasting: A Neural VEC Approach, Neural Network World, 4 (5), 461-471.

Robert, P. Flood and Nancy, P. Marion, 1997. Policy Implications of Second-Generation Crisis models, International Monetary Fund, Staff Papers, 44, 382-390.

Rosenblatt, F, 1958. The Perceptron: A Probabilistic Model for Information Storage and Organization in the Brain, Psych, 65, 386-408.

Rumelhart, D. E., G. E., Hinton and R. J., Williams, 1985. Learning Internal Representation by Error Propagation, Parallel Distributed Processing, 1 (1), 318-326.

Rumelhart, D. E. and McClelland, J. L., 1986. Parallel Distributed Processing: Explorations in the Microstructure of Congition, Vol. 1. Cambridge, MA: MIT Press.

Samata, G. P. and Sanjib, Bordoloi, 2005. Predicting Stock Market-An Application of Artificial Neural Network Technique, Finance India, 19, 173-188.

Scharfstein, David S. and Stein, Jeremy C., 1990. Herd Behavior and Investment, The American Economic Review, 80, 465-479.

Somanath, V. S., 1986. Efficient Exchange Rate Forecasts: Lagged Models Better than the Random Walk, Journal of International Money and Finance, 5, 195-221.

Stornetta, W. S. and Huberman, B. A., 1988. An Improved Three Layered Back-Propagation Algorithm, in Proceedings of the IEEE First International Conference on Neural Network.

Su, Mu-Chun and Zhang, Xian-Dao, 2004. Machine Learning : Neural Network, Fuzzy Systems and Genetic Algorithms, CHWA Publication.

Takagi, T. and Sugeno, M., 1985. Fuzzy Identification of Systems and Its Applications to Modeling and Control, IEEE Transactions on Systems, Man and Cybernetics, 15, 116-132.

Tang, Z.P. and Fishwick, A., 1993. Feedforward Neural Nets as Models for Time Series Forecasting, ORSA J. Computing, 5, 374-385.

Tatsuyoshi, Miyakoshi, 2000. The Causes of the Asian Currency Crisis: Empirical Observations, Japan and the World Economy, 12, 243-253.

Tzeng, Chun-Hsien, 1999. The Stability of Euro. Graduate Institute of International Business, National Taiwan University, Taiwan. (In Chinese)

Van, Rijcheghem C. and Weder, B., 1999. Financial Contagion: Spillovers through Banking Centers [Mimeo], IMF.

Weibel, A., Hanazawa, T., Hinton, G., Shikano, K. and Lang, K., 1989. Phenomena Recognition Using Time-Delay Neural Networks. IEEE Transactions on Accoustics, Speech, and Signal Processing, 37, 328-339.

Wu, Iee-Fund and Goo, Yeong-Jia, 2005. A Neuro-Fuzzy Computing Technique for Modeling the Time Series of Short-Term NT$/US$ Exchange rate, Journal of American Academy of Business, 7, 176-181.

Yeh, Po-Tsun, 2002. Forecasting the Exchange Rate by Using Neural Network: An Application to the Euro Dollars. Graduate School of Business Administration, Chung Yuan Christian University, Taiwan. (In Chinese)

Yu, Lean, Wang, Shouyang and Lai, K. K., 2005. A Novel Nonlinear Ensemble Forecasting Model Incorporating GLAR and ANN for Foreign Exchange Rates, Computers & Operations Research, 32, 2523-2541.

Yuko, Hashimoto, 2005. The Impact of the Japanese Banking Crisis on the Intraday FX Market in Late 1997, Journal of Asian Economics, 16, 205-222.

Zadeh, L. A., 1973. Outline of a New Approach to the Analysis of Complex System and Decision Processes, IEEE Transactions on System, Man and Cybernetics, 3(1), 28-44.

Zhang, Aishe and Zhang, Ling, 2004. RBFN Neural Network for the Prediction of Building Interference effects, Computers & Structures, 2333-2339.